Find
Your
Animal

Find Your Animal

A Spiritual Guide to Self-Discovery

Dina Saalisi

Illustrations by Hsiao-Ron Cheng

Laurence King Publishing

Contents

A note from the author

*I'm aware of the concern about cultural appropriation
and the ongoing conversation that this complex topic
presents. That said, I am mindful to recognize and
honor indigenous people and their profound spiritual
practices that relate to animals. As a healer, I utilize various
subtle energies from nature, be it flower, rock, or animal,
in order to guide others in catalyzing greater health and
well-being. I perceive nature as the ultimate healer and as
the one source from which all life emerges and is nourished.
It is within the realm of animals that we as humans reside
and we can set an intention to commune with the various
energies of nature, at will. I invite you to more deeply
explore the connection you share with your fellow animals
and find healing within this magical place.*

How do we listen to animals?

It's quite simple. All life energy is connected. As humans, we perceive this connection through our intellect. With the understanding that everything is made up of molecules and atoms, we can collect and process information about our physical energy. We can also expand this awareness to include our life-force energy or "spirit," which makes up who we are on the inside, at our deepest layer of being. From this inner depth, we can connect with the subtle energy that surrounds us in nature and use it for self-empowerment.

Spiritual healers have known for centuries that energy is exchanged between all life forms, at all times. When we connect with animals energetically, we understand that life energy goes beyond physical form and exists on an invisible level. This abstract quality can also be referred to as "essence." As human animals, we can easily attune to these energies present in our relationships with other mammals, birds, insects, and amphibians. Through awareness of our own inner being, we can utilize the power, wisdom, and support available from the Animal Guides we attract. In this way, we embrace Animal energy as "medicine" for our souls.

Throughout history, all cultures have used animals to symbolize protectors and guides. Ancient Egyptian deities were depicted with the heads of animals that relate to the powers they were thought to possess. Hindu mythology holds sacred animal gods and the lessons they are believed to impart. Buddhism has always subscribed to the idea that all animals are sentient beings, that they possess souls and are meant to be treated with devotion and respect. Celtic traditions recognized a strong connection to animal companions and honored the protection they provided. The ancient arts of qi gong, tai chi, and yoga all emulate animal movements that embody greater physical presence and strength.

Indigenous tribes around the world believed, in one way or another, that animals appearing in dreams or summoned by healers symbolized deeper meanings and imparted wisdom to the individual to whom they became visible. Native American customs including animals were foundational spiritual practices and varied between tribes. Animal "totems" come from the Ojibwe people and relate to a particular animal or set of animals that reflect the characteristics and behaviors of a specific clan. These animals act as spiritual entities that enable deeper reflection and awareness of the mysteries of life. The varied global customs for connecting with animal energy are each unique, yet they all share the same awareness that humans are spiritually related to our wild friends and there is much to be learned from this symbiosis.

Throughout our lives we may encounter several Animal Guides, emerging in different energetic forms, at different times. Each time an Animal Guide appears before us, we can reflect on its specific role in order to recognize the particular functions that it serves.

Power Animals make their presence known throughout the course of our lives or over many years during periods of major transition and growth. Our Power Animals reflect who we are. We share with them habits and characteristics, and recognizing these empowers us to more fully embrace our true nature.

Guardians provide protection in times of need. They may appear by our side on short journeys into places where we feel vulnerable, or their energy may be felt throughout our lives. They can be summoned in moments when courage is called for, creating safety within.

Teachers offer insight into deeper parts of ourselves. They usually appear when we are in need of the illumination of a skillful guide. We can summon them when clarity is called for, in the moment or when reflecting on larger issues.

Messengers appear fleetingly and, usually, unexpectedly. They connect us to deeper meanings through signs, symbols, and omens that pertain to current life challenges. They help us to observe our relationship to the larger world around us.

Refer to the individual Animal descriptions in the main section of this book to understand in which form the animal appears to you and the support that it provides.

How to discover your Power Animals, Guardians, Teachers, and Messengers

Communicating with Animal Guides allows us to embrace the positive influences they provide in order to create greater self-empowerment. There are endless opportunities for uniting with Animal energy. Sometimes simply finding a feather on the beach or noticing pawprints on the hiking trail is enough to make us hear what is calling to be heard. Observing the messages from our Animal couriers helps us uncover answers to many of our complex questions.

As well as noticing how and when Animal Guides greet us and what their presence means, we can also purposely set the intention to create a connection. We trust that the images that appear are being called to emerge from our unconscious minds. It is within this liminal space that we can heed the subtle messages and discover truths about ourselves, which are often hidden from consciousness.

As you begin to connect with your Animal Guides, here are some things to keep in mind:

• Discovering and being led by Animal energy is an exciting journey, which is both enjoyable and profound. Embrace the experience with a sense of curiosity and awe.

- Working with the essence of Animal Guides is an intuitive process. It asks that you trust your inner knowing in order to recognize the signs and symbols that arise.

- Keep a dedicated unlined journal for recording your Animal Guides. Each time you encounter an animal, either in physical or spiritual form, write down your experience in as much detail as possible. You may also sketch the animals to focus your consideration of their physical characteristics. As the moon cycles aid us in activating our inner awareness, re-read your writings on the new and full moon of each month to reflect on your insights and observations. This will help you to make meaning from the power, wisdom, and messages provided by your Animal Guides.

- Whenever you feel particularly drawn to an animal, you can refer to the descriptions in the main section of the book, as a guide to the messages and wisdom this attraction might convey.

The following pages describe some common ways in which Animal Guides might appear to us, and include an intentional guided visualization practice for summoning animal allies, at will. These methods can be used to engage with your Animal Guides when you wish to connect with them for help with a particular challenge, for protection from a specific fear, or for lasting spiritual support.

Feeling a deep connection with the mysteries of nature is our inherent way of being and is the first step in connecting with Animal energy. By simply taking notice of the earth and all of the energy alive in the plants, rocks, waters, soil, and animals, we begin this journey of self-discovery. The easiest way to join with Animal energy is to go out into nature regularly and observe what animals appear before you. You can tune in to their habits, colors, sounds, and scents and engage with the primal energy offered. You can also invite animals into your space by installing bird homes, feeders, and water features and by planting pollinator gardens.

Each time an Animal Guide appears to you in a dream, reflect on the symbols that are presented to you. How do you interact with the animal? Observe the surroundings. Where are you and who else is present? What messages does the animal convey? What does the animal tell you about yourself that you are unable to see in waking hours?

Anyone who has a dog or cat knows of the deep connection and sense of affection they instill. Time spent with our animal friends affords companionship, joy, and continual opportunities for respite and play. Sometimes our pets come to us as if by magic. We might welcome a feral cat that appears on our doorstep into our hearts and homes. Or perhaps a friend or family member gifts us a puppy who becomes a steadfast partner in our lives. More commonly, we choose our pets—or is it more accurate to say that they choose us? When a rescue animal greets us with a wagging tail or lifts a furry paw, we just know that this is the one. Whether by chance or by choice, these animals are particularly dear to us: we call them by affectionate names and include them in our daily routines. Most pet owners find it easy to commune with these comrades. As we naturally look towards them for guardianship and wisdom, we learn much about ourselves through their loving eyes.

When my daughter was quite small, she announced that she was connected with Animal energy and wanted to guide me through discovering my own personal Animal mentor. She sat me down and asked me to close my eyes and think of the first animal that came to mind. Instantly, Bat appeared before me and was dubbed my Animal Guide. I had never before felt connected to Bat energy, yet I accepted this symbol as one worth exploring. As I acquainted myself with the habits and powers of this creature, I could truly feel an embodiment of Bat energy, which continues to lead me to higher truths about myself. Although my daughter's method was quite simple, there is much to be said for trusting our intuition to guide us towards engaging Animal energy.

Meeting your Animal Guides

This visualization practice is more sophisticated than the simple exercise above yet uses the same principle of allowing your intuition to guide you.

Before you begin, you can read it aloud and record it to your phone, so you can do the practice with your eyes closed. Alternately, you can have someone read it to you. Pause for a few moments after reading each bullet point, allowing yourself space to connect deeply with your Animal Guide.

• Begin by closing your eyes and sitting with your feet grounded on the floor, feeling the support of the earth energy beneath you.

• Take several deep breaths, inhaling and exhaling fully and completely. Do this for 5-10 breaths until you feel a sense of calm and inner peace.

• Using your mind's eye, imagine yourself—in your most confident, powerful form—in a place that is magical and tranquil.

• Feel yourself in this beautiful place and notice the sights, sounds, and textures that surround you.

• As you enter more deeply into this sacred space, feel yourself meeting your Animal Guide. See the animal clearly, as it appears before you. Trust that the first image that arises is exactly as it should be.

• Feel yourself strongly drawn into the presence of your Animal Guide. Reflect on the appearance and habits it displays and what meaning you feel these traits convey.

• Welcome its power, protection, wisdom, and messages. Approach your Animal Guide and thank it for being here for you. You may ask it if it has anything to share with you. Accept the first answers that arise as your truths.

- Spend as much time here as you would like, allowing the energy to wash over you, and embrace a sense of empowerment.

- Once you feel complete, thank your Animal Guide and bid it farewell, knowing that you will connect with it again soon and that it is always available to you for support and guidance.

- Take several more full, deep breaths. When you're ready, slowly bring your awareness back to your body, back to the room, and open your eyes, feeling energized and empowered.

Each time you connect with an Animal Guide, use your journal to help you more fully understand the experience. The following questions can be asked:

What traits and habits do
I share with this Animal Guide?

In what other ways are this
Animal Guide and I connected?

What messages does this
Animal Guide have for me?

Where do I see myself led to when
I follow this Animal Guide's advice?

What holds me back from following
this Animal Guide's advice?

How can this Animal Guide
help me to move forward?

The following are descriptions of 40 Animal Guides and what their presence means when they appear in your life. Reflect on the power, protection, wisdom, and messages provided by each Animal Guide.

Coyote

Juxtaposition, Equilibrium,
Communication

C oyote is one of the most adaptable animals in the
world. Government programs have been enacted to
try to eradicate this stealthy creature, considered a pest by
wildlife officials, yet it persists and has actually grown in
numbers, expanding its habitats to include regions of North
America that were originally Coyote-free. A wily character
indeed, Coyote creates homes in hillsides, gulches, and
canyons or takes over the existing dens of smaller animals.
And if anyone disturbs the lair, it will take its young and
find accommodations elsewhere. The father, as well as the
mother, plays a significant role in raising the pups. For those
who have Coyote as their Animal, this can be seen in a
close-knit family structure and a harmonious home life.

We cannot reflect on Coyote behavior without recognition
of its eerie vocal abilities. From dusk 'til dawn, the barks, yips,
and howls can be heard echoing far and wide, alerting kin to
its whereabouts or threatening prey. It is this distinctive call
that makes Coyote presence felt and feared. The lesson, then,
is to become able to transform external clamor into internal
empowerment, through more conscious communication.

In North American indigenous lore Coyote is known
as the trickster. As an Animal Guide, Coyote appears at
times to show us when things aren't what they might seem.
We may be able to sense a contradiction, for example feeling
mistrust of someone who appears honorable—opposites
showing us our inner truths. We can reflect on our lives
and see how we are being insincere in our dealings or,
conversely, we can see how we are being treated unfairly

by others. Do we tend to let others down after making promises? Do we tend to make excuses for others when they don't live up to their end of the bargain?

Anytime Coyote energy is present there is always a dual meaning to our experience. What seems like a wise choice may be foolish under closer examination. And the opposite is true. What seems silly may have deeper meaning that we are not able to see at first. As we connect with Coyote energy, we become empowered to see the truths behind the façade and to enjoy life in ways that are balanced with discernment and wisdom.

Power

- You are able to achieve balance in work and play. Flexibility is natural for you, moving between projects, ideas, and tasks with fluidity and ease.

- You have the ability to discern what needs to be done and you are able to skillfully carry out your plans. Cooperation is a tool with which you are quite familiar.

- You desire to be part of a close-knit family or group of friends, for life. You are loyal and enjoy the camaraderie in having loved ones share in fun experiences.

- Nighttime and early morning are the most productive times for you. Use this time to reflect on what it is you truly wish to be creating and with whom.

- Those who embrace Coyote as their Animal make excellent leaders, as well as adroit team players.

Protection

◆ Be cautious of those who seem "too good to be true." Are they promising something they can't provide? Notice when others say one thing, then do another. Remember that you can use your vocal power to speak your truth when you notice inconsistency or insincerity in others.

Wisdom

◆ Strive for balance in all areas of life. Are you being honest with yourself about your current relationships and endeavors? Are there people whom you are putting your faith in who don't deserve it?

◆ Notice when you tend to procrastinate and how this shows up in your current affairs. Laziness can feel overwhelming at times. When this happens, take yourself outside and walk barefoot on the earth. Allow yourself to feel alive inside life's rhythms and embrace a sense of equilibrium from this support.

Messages from Coyote

When Coyote arrives, look for
the dualities that are present in your life.

Watch out for excessive doing, which leads
to fatigue and burnout, or conversely, spending too
much time in leisure without tending to your work.

Are you taking things too seriously?
Observe the humor in the situation at hand.

See the challenge through the eyes of a child.

Bison

Generosity, Boldness, Spirituality

O ne of the largest land mammals on the planet, weighing up to 2,000 lbs (900 kg), with an ability to reach speeds of 35 mph (56 kph), Bison exhibits boldness like no other. Although typically gentle in demeanor, a herbivore who prefers to be left alone, Bison may turn forceful when scared or aroused. As an Animal Guide, this behavior reflects a forward nature beneath a passive façade. Those who embrace Bison energy often surprise others with their sudden brashness, as they appear quiet and reserved upon first meeting. The lesson provided by this soulful guide is to learn to temper zeal with inner peace.

Bison supplied more necessities for early humans than any other animal in North American history. Indigenous people used the entirety of its body for food, clothing, shelter, tools, and fuel. In this vital ability to provide, we can see the generosity displayed in this Animal Guide. Sadly, this partnership was disrupted by settlers, which led to the creature's near-demise. Yet the spirit of Bison lives on indomitably in stories, lore, and our souls. As an Animal Guide, this powerful being leads us to a place of kindness within ourselves that can be shared with others and will remain strong, even after we're gone.

Bison is larger than life, an almost mythical creature. Most humans alive today have never encountered Bison in the wild, yet we are familiar with tales of when this beautiful beast roamed the earth. When we reflect on the powerful Bison essence that prevails, we can see this as a deep communion with an ethereal soul. Bison encourages us to explore parts of ourselves that are hidden from consciousness, to be revealed in dreams and on spiritual journeys. Bison is a terrestrial creature profoundly affected by the rhythms of nature; those who hold Bison energy trust in the truths found within the mysteries of symbolism and inner knowing.

Bison has always been associated with spirituality, and the indigenous peoples of the Plains showed reverence and gratitude for the gifts lavished by this great animal. There were special prayers and elaborate rituals to honor the sacred relationship between Bison and human. When we look towards this peaceful being for guidance, we are led to profound self-awareness through spiritual processes. Bison makes excellent medicine for anyone who wishes to deepen their exploration of esoteric and spiritual studies.

Power

- You are shy when meeting others for the first time. Once you feel comfortable, you become bold in your self-expression.

- You have a big heart and enjoy sharing your gifts.

- You are a strong and capable being, and others look towards you for wisdom and support.

- You are drawn to alternative spiritual practices. Bison souls enjoy learning about metaphysical subjects, nature, energy healing, crystals, and herbs.

- Deeply in tune with the rhythms of the earth, you trust your intuition implicitly.

Protection

- When feeling burdened by your commitments, allow yourself to slow down and prioritize your needs. Ensure enough time for self-nourishment and creativity.

- When you notice yourself being overly analytical, connect with your inner knowing. Trust whatever arises as your truth.

- In order to create more balance in your life, join with the earth often. Regularly go out into nature to hike, swim, or garden.

Wisdom

- A generous soul knows no bounds.

- Balance strength with peace. Through equilibrium you emerge as the truly powerful being you are.

- Let the earth be your guide.

- You have everything you need and more.

Messages from Bison

Reflect on your current spiritual practices. Are you allowing yourself enough time to cultivate your intuition? Create space that allows your inner voice to be heard and honored.

When Bison enters your realm, recognize your needs in a new light. Rather than putting yourself at the end of the line, begin each day by giving yourself what you need to thrive.

Now is a powerful time to join with the earth. Dig in the dirt. Start a garden. If you don't have a yard, join a community garden or add houseplants to each room in your home and office.

Horse

Dependability, Adventure, Strength

One of the domestic animals with which humans enjoy a deep connection, Horse is a robust creature that guides us towards our passion for adventure. Domesticated in lands north of the Black and Caspian seas 5,000 years ago, Horse has always been a companion for those traveling to new lands. As an Animal Guide, it symbolizes an ability to freely explore the parts of ourselves that are in need of revival. This powerful being helps us to recognize our inner strength and understand how to activate it in order to advance in life. Those who embrace Horse as a teacher are the bold ones, who carry themselves with a certainty about where they are headed and the fearlessness to get them there.

Horses and humans worldwide enjoy a profound relationship, a spiritual bond grounded in the stability of the earth. We can see this reflected in the way a rider magically conveys directions based on subtle body movements, and Horse responds by performing exactly as expected, in a beautiful dance of dependability. Horse as an Animal Guide denotes an ability to be there for others in times of need, as a steadfast companion through challenging periods of life. We can honor this gift within ourselves and generously share it with others.

The mighty presence of Horse is a universal symbol of fortitude and virility. We observe Horse energy in those who are naturally gifted athletes, or in anyone who uses their strength as an asset in physical endeavors. These are the stars of the soccer team, the award-winning gymnasts, or the multi-lap swimmers. When we witness an agile body coupled with a powerful stature, we can be sure that this Animal leads the way.

These gentle giants survive solely on plant-based diets. Their robust physicality is balanced by a gentle heart, which yields to the commands of their rider. This profound connection is illustrated perfectly when we observe the duo galloping along as one entity. Horse as an Animal Guide allows us to embrace our ability to enjoy relationships, from a place of selfless offering.

Power

• An adventurous soul, you love to travel and are always curious to explore new places.

• Strength and fortitude are displayed in your physique.

• You have a gift for self-reflection, as you fearlessly confront your challenges head-on.

• You are dependable by nature, which makes you a reliable friend and colleague. Others often regard you as a steadfast guide.

• You are a generous being who is able to selflessly give to others.

Protection

• When you feel restless, consider a visit to a new place that you've always wanted to explore. Take a walk in a local garden, drop by a used bookstore, or plan a trip to an exotic location.

• At times you may feel incapable of completing tasks that seem too physically strenuous. Take it slow. Connect with your gifts of somatic endurance, grounded in sharp intellect, and proceed with confidence.

Wisdom

- Embrace your daring spirit. Ride like the wind. Roam as you please.

- Strong and sturdy, your body will carry you far. Believe in your power of endurance.

- The more you are able to give, the greater the gifts you will receive in return.

Messages from Horse

When Horse gallops into your life, reflect on how you support others. Are you shirking responsibilities? Connect with your capacity for dependability in order to offer your services in a more reliable way.

Observe your current state of health. Assess your diet and exercise routine to see how you can revise them to develop greater well-being.

Now is a good time to plan that trip you've been dreaming about. Research your options, gather your resources, and set an intention to embark on the journey.

Hummingbird

Nourishment, Freedom, Joy

T he smallest of all birds, Hummingbird holds a special
place in nature as a tiny, yet mighty, being. There are
over 300 species native to the Americas and the Caribbean
islands, and their supernatural beauty and grace have
garnered them much acclaim worldwide. The symbol of
Hummingbird has been used for centuries in design, as
it relates to a sense of mystical beauty. Most indigenous
tribes of the New World regarded Hummingbird energy
as spiritual and significant in their rituals. Pueblo women
favored Hummingbird for its feathers, which were said to
hold magical powers for promoting love. When Hummingbird
enters your life, you can be sure that you will receive the
blessings of beauty and love.

Just observing this tiny creature at work and play is
exhausting. This astounding creature buzzes and hums, as it
beats its wings at an incredibly high frequency. By rotating
its wings in a figure-eight pattern, Hummingbird is the only
bird that can hover in mid-air. A male will soar to dizzying
heights and swoop straight down to impress a female, but this
acrobatic feat in no way denotes a partnership. Hummingbird
is a fiercely independent soul, and those who recognize this
being as their Animal typically prefer to fly solo, whirring
along from adventure to adventure.

We cannot reflect on Hummingbird energy without
contemplating their beneficial symbiotic relationship with
flowers. One can't survive without the other. The birds eat
50-60 meals per day, consisting mostly of the nectar from
fresh blossoms. As they do so, they transfer pollen throughout
the garden, thus generating more flowers. In those who have
Hummingbird as their Animal, this speaks to the ability to

drink in the deliciousness of life, while continually creating plentiful sources of nourishment. Not only are we able to offer ourselves the sustenance we need for survival, but we can also choose to experience all of the wondrous joys around us.

Playfulness is a theme that emerges when Hummingbird energy is near. Reveling in pleasure and delight, those who embrace this Animal have a natural proclivity for whatever feeds the soul. Darting from elation to elation, one is reminded to take adequate time for rest and replenishment. By creating balance in all things, we are then able to savor joy and truly live life to its fullest.

Power

◆ You possess a playful nature with a deep appreciation for the beauty of life, and often experience boundless joy.

◆ You regularly enjoy time for nourishment and self-care.

◆ You have a natural ability for working with flowers. Hummingbird power is present in those who are gardeners, herbalists, flower-essence therapists, and aromatherapists.

◆ You cherish your independence. You are the most productive when working alone.

◆ Your high energy and deft skills allow you to accomplish a lot within a short amount of time.

Protection

◆ Trust in your inner strength to nourish you when you feel depleted. Allow Hummingbird energy to feed you the nectar of life to create replenishment.

◆ A powerful medicine for sorrow and depression, this Animal guardian connects you to the inherent joy that is alive within.

◆ Whenever you feel unsure about how to expend your energy, call on Hummingbird to direct you to your true passions.

Wisdom

• Embrace the positive in all experiences.

• Beauty is everywhere. Pause often. Take notice.
Feed your soul.

• Consistency with self-care practices creates
empowerment and inner strength.

• Balance your work with time to simply enjoy life and play!

Messages from Hummingbird

When Hummingbird emerges, pause and
reflect on your personal-nourishment routine.
Are you in need of replenishment?
Give yourself time to engage in mindfulness practices
that benefit your body, mind, spirit, and soul.

Are you feeling impatient and rushed?
Hummingbird asks that you slow down.

Notice your balance of work and play.
Make efforts to seek more joy in all that you do.

Observe your home and the spaces around you.
Is it time to redecorate or plant a garden?

Whenever Hummingbird appears,
know that you are entering a powerful cycle of life.
Get ready for the ride!

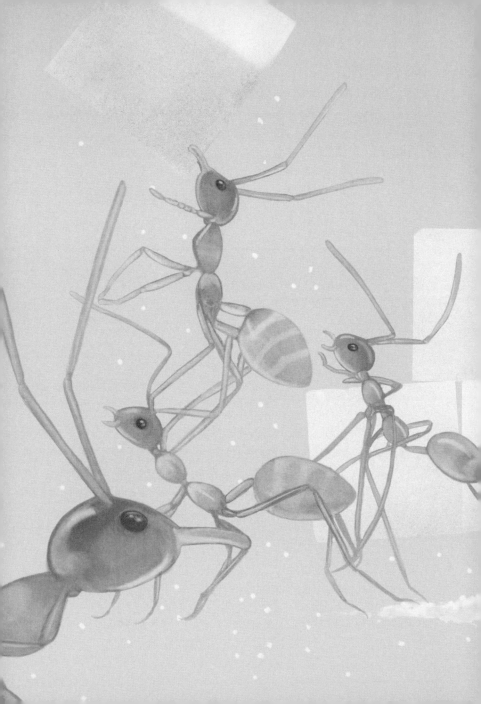

Ant

Socialization, Stamina, Complexity

Estimated to comprise at least 10 percent of the entire animal population, Ant ranks as one of the most widespread species in the world. For more than a hundred million years this curious creature has played an important role in the survival of the ecosystem. From turning soil to limiting invasive pests, the skills displayed by this creature make an enormous contribution to the well-being of the planet. Those who embrace Ant care deeply about the natural world and work diligently to honor and preserve it.

Although individually insignificant, working together as an army of hundreds of thousands, usually governed by one queen, Ant possesses the power of teamwork like no other creature. Tirelessly toiling away, the individuals in a colony use their energy to the benefit of all, rather than solely for self. This evolved socialization structure signifies an ability to thrive within community connection, and Ant wisdom is displayed in those who join with others in collaborative creativity. Each solitary being bestows its independent expertise in order to develop a greater outcome than could be achieved alone. The guidance offered by Ant energy is one of collective power, which beautifully displays the concept of strength in numbers.

Ant's curious attributes include "sleeping" for approximately 8 minutes every 12 hours, extraordinary communication through pheromones, and the ability to build intricate multi-roomed homes. In an Animal Guide these traits denote an ability to achieve successful outcomes using a collection of unusual skills.

Small and mighty is indeed the essence of Ant. One of the tiniest animals on the planet, Ant can lift objects weighing 50 times its own body weight. We've all witnessed these complicated creatures carrying pieces of food effortlessly across the room. Those who regard Ant as their Animal are blessed with immense stamina. They employ unconventional means, coupled with indefatigable skills, to bring their dreams to fruition.

Power

• You are a hard worker and at times find it difficult to slow down.

• You feel most empowered when working in a group and often partner with others to develop strong communities.

• Naturally gifted in the language of the earth, you understand the needs of the planet and are conscientious about its preservation. Ant medicine makes skilled stewards of the land, such as gardeners, conservationists, farmers, and healers.

• You are a complex individual and display many unusual characteristics. Others find your enigmatic qualities awe-inspiring.

• You possess great physical strength and sense of purpose, which makes it easy for you to realize your goals.

Protection

• When you are daunted by the tasks on your to-do list, call on friends and neighbors to pitch in. In return, offer your help on their projects. By drawing on the various skills of each person, you are forming the foundation for a strong community.

• To keep your reserves of energy up, allow yourself to take breaks often throughout the day. Set a timer to remind you to pause. Take a short walk, read a magazine, or eat a healthy snack. Return to your work with newfound strength.

Wisdom

- A mighty being on the inside, allow your power to emerge and lead you towards your ultimate goals.

- Diligence in all you do affords time for relaxation.

- Find strength in those who surround you.

- You are capable of achieving your greatest desires.

Messages from Ant

Your hard work is paying off.
You will soon see the positive results of your
persistent pursuit of a long-term goal.

Are you doing your share to contribute to
the greater good? When Ant creeps into your life,
reflect on your community commitments.

Has life become too complicated?
Evaluate ways in which you might scale
back obligations in order to give yourself
more time for replenishment.

Frog
Consciousness, Fertility, Generational Healing

With an ability to live both in and out of water, this creature displays a deep connection to the enchanting energies of the moon and water. Frog leads us to knowledge of our fertile inner existence. Those who embrace Frog as their Animal are at home with their emotions and aren't afraid to express them clearly and openly.

When we listen to the wisdom of this vocal Animal Guide we can hark back to our ancient roots. Its teachings encourage us to dig deep within the murky challenges of life and cull the productive solutions that are waiting to emerge.

In this Animal Guide's connection to the primordial waters of life, we recognize the metaphor for rich abundance. Frog guides us towards our wellspring within and helps us to access our ancient wisdom. From here, we can share our divine knowing and contribute to our ancestral healing, which in turn creates the continual renewal of humanity. Those who are led by Frog energy are on a path of transcendent growth and supreme consciousness.

Frog enjoys hopping from one interest to another, which makes for a colorful individual with many talents and gifts. The practice, then, is to stay focused and present and not to whittle away precious moments in folly. Frog is here to teach us how to best serve ourselves, in each moment. This is reflected in our ability to make to-do lists, stick to schedules, and initiate and complete projects with ease.

The symphony of Frog serenades on a warm evening can easily lull us into a peaceful state. As we relax into the harmonies, we bear witness to these creatures working together to speak a larger truth than one could convey alone. In this way, we can regard Frog as a guide in strengthening the communication skills of the collective consciousness of humanity. As we give voice to our unified messages with more clarity, they can be received with greater acceptance.

Power

+ You possess a deep connection to the spiritual wisdom of your ancient roots.

+ You are an excellent communicator and you are adept at balancing your tone of voice to optimize reception.

+ A deeply emotional soul, yours is the way of feeling.

+ Frog energy makes for excellent vocalists and public speakers.

Protection

+ When you notice that time seems to be slipping through your fingers and you don't feel motivated to complete your tasks, take a moment to create a schedule that you can adhere to.

+ When challenging emotions rise to the surface, allow yourself the time and space to process them with loving acceptance.

Wisdom

+ Speak your mind from the depths of your soul.

+ Plant seeds for future generations. Trust in the spiritual growth of the planet.

+ From the depths of ancient waters come the gifts of profound healing.

Messages from Frog

Do you feel lazy and unproductive?
Do you feel anxious,
jumping from one project to the next?
Frog energy is available to help you
bring balance to your schedule.

Notice your communication habits.
Are you able to reach others with a melodic voice?
Or are your words coming out harshly?

When Frog emerges, take time
to delve into the depths of your soul.
Listen to beautiful music, read poetry,
or walk in nature.

Ladybug
Positivity, Ascension, Luck

O riginally dubbed the "ladybird beetle" in seventeenth-century England, this delightful insect is equated with good fortune everywhere in the world. Childhood rhymes herald the magical luck following the appearance of Ladybug and we've all had the experience of feeling blessed when this mystical being lands on us, as we close our eyes and make a wish. Ladybug takes flight, carries our wishes into the universe, and brings them to fruition. One story, from China, tells of the arrival of Ladybug as a prophecy of new love—the number of spots signifying the number of months one must wait for the joyous occurrence.

A natural guardian, Ladybug creates a sense of safety as well as good fortune. Her role in the garden is to protect against pest invasions and ensure the health and longevity of the plants. As an Animal Guide, this enigmatic creature gladly offers this protection to those who ask. Creating an energetic shield to block out misfortune, her power is both charming and fierce. Invasive challengers beware! This defender banishes negativity and swiftly combats whatever invites it. When we're surrounded by pessimism, we can counter it with the positivity Ladybug provides. The wisdom of Ladybug, as both a predator and a pollinator, contains a duality. Alleviating what causes destruction and encouraging what creates empowerment are natural talents of this nimble creature.

Those who are fortunate enough to connect with Ladybug energy gladly share the abundance of their blessings with others. A natural-born giver, Ladybug reminds us that it is through this harmony that we create the conditions for living a joyful life. A keen understanding of this exchange of energy helps us to continue this successful flow.

Power

- You were born under a lucky star. Ladybug as an Animal Guide makes for a blessed existence, free from hardship and struggle.

- Naturally gifted with powers of protection, those who carry Ladybug energy have a sense of confidence and safety in all their endeavors.

- You have an ability to clearly recognize your desires and a knack for creating the conditions to bring them to fruition.

- You are a joyful soul who creates well-being in your environment and brings merriment to those around you.

- Those who embrace Ladybug as their Animal make excellent life coaches and mentors.

Protection

- If misfortune comes your way, embrace your ability to rise above whatever challenges you.

- When toxic energies shroud your environment, you can create a protective boundary to ward off negativity.

- You have the ability to make what you desire a reality. Do you know what it is that you truly want? Before making any requests, reflect on your deeper hopes and dreams to proceed with more clarity.

Wisdom

◆ Wishes do come true! Set your intentions for positive outcomes. Expect your desires to be fulfilled.

◆ Don't let anything stand in the way of realizing your dreams.

◆ Tune in to the abundance that is all around you.

◆ Practice patience. Trust that your dreams will be made manifest, when the timing is right.

Messages from Ladybug

You are entering a cycle of good fortune
and abundance. Challenges are passing out
of your life, as newfound joys emerge.
Use this powerful time to connect with what
may have previously felt out of reach.

Reflect on the energy that surrounds you.
Are you letting negativity creep in?
What can you do to strengthen your boundaries?

When Ladybug has landed in your life,
ask for what you desire and allow yourself to
receive the blessings of this magical Animal Guide.
Your wishes will be granted.
All you have to do is ask.

Wolf

Intuition, Collaboration, Voice

W hen we think of Wolf, we conjure images of a sly
creature that behaves in antisocial ways. The "big bad
wolf" is a sinister figure in children's stories and becomes
even more terrifying in legends about the werewolf, the man
who turns into a monster at the full moon. Wolf's fearsome
reputation reflects its voracious appetite for prey. Yet there
are other fables that hold Wolf as a benevolent guide in the
midst of challenges, as in the Roman myth of Romulus and
Remus, where the abandoned twins are found and cared
for by a she-wolf. This symbolizes Wolf as a guardian that
appears in times of need.

Mammals always signify a profound connection to earth
energy, as they walk on the ground, absorbing the essence of
life. Wolf is no exception. Deeply intuitive, this being is able to
connect with the mysteries of the world and transmute them
into earnest wisdom. Wolf as an Animal Guide symbolizes
a deep appreciation for nature and an understanding of how
to interact within this realm to create strong connections.
Social animals living in packs, they join together to hunt,
as well as to play. This trait symbolizes extraordinary gifts for
collaboration and camaraderie.

Wolf was once thought to be extinct in parts of North
America and Europe, but an effort to build a home for them
in Yellowstone National Park over 25 years ago has helped
bring their numbers back up. Wolf travels far and fast.
Packs cover many miles of terrain each day and can run at
a pace of up to 25 mph (40 kph) or faster over short distances.
Using intellect and swift skill, Wolf hunts and devours until
it can hold no more, then returns to the den to revel in the
comforts of family and home. Wolf partners mate for life,

which denotes an ability to care for loved ones from a place of loyalty and devotion. Those who welcome this attentive Animal Guide make kindhearted family members and friends.

An immense vocal ability is a gift this wise one shares. Wolf uses clamorous calls to alert other members of a hunt, or may give a "lonesome howl" to let others know it has been isolated from the group. Those who embrace Wolf energy are talented singers and speakers. When this messenger has arrived in your life, reflect on what you would like to express vocally. Have you been holding yourself back from speaking your truth?

Power

- You are instinctually connected with the energy of the earth. Use your intuition to guide you to your highest truths.

- You enjoy socializing with close friends and family. Others appreciate your gift for bringing people together.

- You are fond of traveling to new destinations and are usually the one who assembles group activities and trips.

- You especially appreciate collaboration and often seek out partners for creative and work projects.

- You are talented in conveying your wisdom to others through the spoken word. Wolf energy makes for excellent singers, poets, and public speakers.

Protection

- When seeking answers to questions about the mysteries of life, use your refined powers of intuition.

- In order to find a sense of safety, rely on your instincts to guide you to the places that feel secure.

- When loneliness strikes, reach out to those close to you for connection and support.

Wisdom

- The answers are always available. Look within.

- Trust your intuition and speak your truth.

- There is strength in numbers. Know that you are never alone.

Messages from Wolf

Have you been isolating yourself lately?
Pick up the phone and call on a friend to join
you for a hike, or a chat over a cup of tea.

When Wolf emerges, reflect on what you
know to be true. Allow yourself quietude
in order to hear the small voice inside.

Are you expressing yourself clearly?
Practice asking for what you need with
calmness and clarity, rather than from
a place of anger or fear.

Hawk

Vision, Purpose, Vigilance

Hawk has always been a symbol of dynamic vision. The presence of Hawk as an Animal Guide asks us to become more aware of our experiences. When this being emerges, it signals a time for deep reflection and to honor what we know to be true. From this place of visionary insight, we can touch our truths and shift our point of view to create enlightenment within ourselves, as well as for others.

Blessed with the gift of incredibly sharp sight, Hawk can spot its prey from half a mile away. Continually on guard, this animal is vigilant in obtaining whatever it most desires. When this creature has entered your life, you can be sure that you will become acutely aware of your purpose and will be able to act accordingly to achieve your highest aim.

A natural-born guardian, Hawk will be by your side always once it enters your life. Most species of Hawk mate for life, while both the males and females care for their young, and may inhabit the same nests for years. These traits, combined with incredible hunting skills, symbolize a deep connection to family and an extraordinary ability to provide shelter and sustenance. Those who embrace Hawk as their Animal have a deep desire to create security and nourishment for their loved ones.

Hawk energy rises slowly, becoming activated with age. We may recognize a connection with this Animal Guide but our power becomes manifest only once we've grown through the various stages of life. As we become truly able to grasp the lessons that we've been taught, we can then ascend to new heights of awareness.

As an animal that has an incredible capacity for soaring to the peak of experience, Hawk leads us in the direction of spiritual flourishing through widening our horizons.

Power

• You have a gift of keen inner vision and can see what eludes most others. Those who hold Hawk as their Animal are excellent counselors, leaders, and intuitive thinkers, ready to guide others to higher perspectives with clarity and ease.

• You enjoy providing for your family and creating a loving home.

• Fearless by nature, you are unafraid to stand up to anyone who challenges you.

• You have a strong sense of self and you know what you are capable of.

• You are adept at practicing patience. Your vigilance pays off, as you invariably sail away with the prize.

Protection

• As you reach for higher levels of success, are you fearful of not achieving your goals? Call upon Hawk to help you re-evaluate whatever you wish to attain.

• When you are feeling uncertain, take time to go inward to receive the answers you are seeking.

• When Hawk emerges as a guardian, its presence can be felt as a sense of constancy. The security provided is one that will span lifetimes.

Wisdom

- Your belief in yourself will carry you far.
  Trust that you already have the answers inside.

- Inner vision is a strength that grows over time.

- Distance gives perspective.

Messages from Hawk

Reflect on how you engage with others
and be cautious of exercising your power over those
who are weaker than you. Are you being too harsh?
How can you find ways to soften your expression?

Take notice of what is going on around you.
Through your keen inner vision, reflect on
how you can realign your energies in order
to make your visions manifest.

It's time to change your perspective
on a current situation. What can you do differently
to bring about your desired results?

Fox

Adaptability, Awareness, Mysticism

"Sly as a fox" is a comparison we've all heard before. With powers of cunning adaptability, Fox has succeeded as one of the most widespread wild carnivores worldwide. This animal knows when to retreat and blend with the surrounding area, giving it a reputation as a "shapeshifter." Those who regard Fox as their Animal enjoy keeping a low profile, as a source of protection. The flip side to this is an acute vulnerability, which, when wielded powerfully, is transformed into a strength rather than experienced as weakness.

Many cultures tell stories of the mystical qualities associated with Fox. Native American traditions regard Fox as the bringer of fire, with profound healing abilities. The Celts believed that the pelts held significant value as a charm containing the magic of insight and inner wisdom. We can reflect on this energy in Fox as an Animal Guide to develop our inner knowing, through deeper spiritual practices.

Fox runs tirelessly at a trot for miles on end, is incredibly light on its feet, and is even able to run up trees when threatened. Those who possess Fox essence are imbued with graceful strength and may enjoy running marathons, eclectic forms of dance, yoga, and martial arts.

Hunted by humans for centuries, Fox has been able to evade capture owing to its shy nature. This denotes a cautious demeanor in relating with others. As we reflect on this, we sense the presence of an extreme vulnerability. Those who embrace this Animal are emotionally sensitive and, when they are able to display this sensitivity freely, can find deep connection in relationships. Fox females are monogamous creatures, create comfortable homes, and make excellent mothers, devoted to their young for the first two months of life. At the same time, they are independent, as they spend nearly half of the year solo. Those who embrace Fox as their Animal enjoy deep commitments, balanced with ample time alone.

Power

- From an early age you became aware of your metaphysical gifts of clairaudience and clairvoyance. You pick up on subtle frequencies and can deeply understand others, as well as messages in nature.

- You are a natural-born problem solver, as you are able to use your wit to overcome obstacles.

- Shy by nature, you have an uncanny ability to make yourself inconspicuous when uncomfortable.

- You are endowed with supreme grace and agility.

Protection

- When entering unknown territory, proceed with caution. Use your powers of cunning to take command and create safety.

- When you feel nervous or shy, use your powerful ability to blend in with your surroundings. This helps you to feel at ease in public and in social situations.

Wisdom

- From vulnerability comes true strength.

- Cunning and wit are surefire ways to success.

- Embrace the rhythms of your body. Play hard. Rest lavishly. Create balance.

Messages from Fox

When Fox enters your realm,
listen for the subtle cues around you, in order
to obtain answers to puzzling problems.

Proceed with caution in business dealings and in
collaborative efforts. Reflect on the situation at hand
and use your acute perceptions to guide you.

Allow yourself to be vulnerable and display
your softer side. Trust your intuitive awareness,
as you express yourself more freely.

Reflect on your present physical state.
Are you getting enough exercise? Are you overdoing it?
Use this awareness to guide you towards a new workout
regime, balanced with time for rest and replenishment.

When Fox pays a visit, reflect on your current
challenges through the lens of intuition.

Owl

Wisdom, Insight, Magic

A deep mysticism envelops Owl. Commonly referred to as a "creature of the night," it can see and hear keenly in complete darkness. An extraordinary hunter, it silently glides, swiftly swoops and grabs prey. Owl swallows its victims whole and coughs up the undigested bones and fur. This symbolizes an ability to take in what others are feeling with keen perception, process it with deep insight, and release what's unnecessary and unwanted. If Owl has emerged in your life, you likely have a sixth sense for understanding others and seeing through illusion.

Owl energy is expressed as magic, prophecy, and clairvoyance. Whenever this Animal Guide appears as a teacher, we can tune in to our inner knowing and allow it to lead us into the deeper mysteries of life. A strictly nocturnal creature, Owl lives in the darkness and has a strong connection with the moon. It is within this sphere of light-filled essence that magic is made. The appearance of Owl as an Animal Guide is a sure sign that we are capable of empowerment through otherworldly realms.

Owl guides us into the depths of our being in order to illuminate the truths within. As an Animal Guide, Owl acts as a guardian in the darkness and helps us to rise above challenges and arrive at a place of newfound wisdom. This is reflected beautifully in myths and lore that hold this majestic bird as a devoted companion. In Greek mythology, Athena, goddess of wisdom and war, kept an Owl on her shoulder to provide her with insight and knowledge of how to secure victory in battle. Hecate, goddess of magic, had Owl for a guardian, as she entered the underworld to perform deep healing rites. Stories such as those of Merlin and Harry Potter illustrate the profound connection that Owl has with healers, magicians, witches, and wizards.

Owl features regularly in North American folklore. The Pawnee revered Owl as a symbol of protection, while the Pueblo associated its power with the transformation of death and rebirth. In Celtic mythology Owl symbolized the underworld and could illuminate submerged truths. As we reflect on this symbolism, we can surely see a thread that weaves together regeneration and inner knowing. Each of these relates to touching the depths of our soul in order to reach insights that we wouldn't otherwise be able to grasp in the light of day.

Power

* You are blessed with the gift of acute inner vision and are connected to otherworldly realms.

* Your especially keen insight gives you an ability to perceive what others cannot.

* You are skilled at hearing what others convey through your innate powers of clairvoyance and intuition.

* You are attracted to the magical arts and possess an ability to work within the depths of human nature in order to create deeper understanding and healing.

* Those who hold Owl as their Animal make excellent teachers, therapists, and healers.

Protection

* At times, your heightened sensitivity may attract unwanted energies from others. When you notice this, you can create an invisible boundary to block negative forces.

* When you feel heavy-hearted you can practice gratitude as a way to alleviate the gloom.

* Use your inner light to flood the darkness of your challenges.

Wisdom

* Observe the deeper meanings in all your experiences.

* Allow yourself to assimilate what is nourishing and release what is not.

* You are strongly connected to psychic energy. To activate this power to its fullest, use the cycles of the moon and dreams to enact deep healing work. Keep a dream journal and re-read your writings on the new and full moon of each month.

Messages from Owl

The arrival of Owl signifies mystery and the unknown.

When Owl appears, listen carefully for unspoken truths.

Closely observe the signs
and symbols that arise in your dreams.

Tune in to your deeper awareness and trust in
your intuition. What do you know to be true?

Whale

Greatness, Depth, Service

Whale is the largest animal that has ever existed. The largest of all species, the Blue Whale, measures up to 100 ft (30 m) long and weighs 330,000 lbs (150 tonnes)! Whale was once considered fearsome, as it fought back against its hunters, but most humans have now developed a more sympathetic understanding of the animal. This Animal Guide teaches us about humility in our relationships. As we learn to practice mutual respect with others, we form bonds through a sense of camaraderie and our faith in humanity is restored.

Early tribal people cultivated a partnership with Whale through reverence and sustainability, using all parts of the animal as food, shelter, tools, or talismans. In Whale as an Animal Guide, this symbolizes a habit of offering unconditional support to our loved ones, with an ability to convey empathy. Those who possess Whale energy are tried and true friends who go out of their way to provide nourishment to others.

An extraordinary soul, Whale continues to perplex scientists with its songs, which invoke a complex language. Mysterious and melodious, the meaning of these communications eludes humans. In the Animal Guide, this denotes a powerful ability to express ourselves from a place of higher intellect. Those who hold Whale as a guide use their deepest wisdom to convey what they know to be true.

Anyone who has ever witnessed Whale during its yearly migration can feel awe for this mighty animal. As large as two city buses, this magnificent powerhouse emerges effortlessly from the waves and rides the surf with intensity.

When we reflect on this massive creature dancing on the sea, we recognize this as an ability to connect with life-force energy from a place of unbridled vigor. Whale teaches us how to enliven our physical power through a strong connection with the ever-changing essence of life. This mystical Animal Guide bestows the gift of being able to gracefully go with the flow.

Power

• You emanate dynamic energy grounded in physical grace.

• Your larger-than-life presence creates a splash wherever you go.

• You are a steadfast friend and are of unconditional service to those you love.

• You possess an extraordinary ability to reach others through your gift of profound vocalization.

• A truly soulful being, yours is the way of depth within the waters of life.

• Those who embrace Whale energy make wonderful performers and athletes.

Protection

• When you feel small and find yourself stuck in self-doubt, reflect inwardly in order to connect with your greatness. Allow this empowerment to guide you forward with confidence.

• Use your depth of communication to reach the ears and souls of others, in order to clarify complex ideas and inspirations.

Wisdom

* Convey wisdom from the depths of your soul.

* As you bestow your gifts on those you love, you cultivate deep connections.

* Balance physical power with grace.

* Allow your greatness to fully emerge.

Messages from Whale

The arrival of Whale asks that you take a dive into the depths of your relationships and assess the ways in which you offer support to others. Are you providing all that you can? Or, are you giving too much of yourself?

Now is the perfect time to evaluate your current physical needs. Reset your diet and exercise regime to develop greater strength and endurance.

When Whale emerges, reflect on your soul journey. How can you reflect on the intensity of your experience, in order to create more awareness?

Mountain Lion

Stamina, Courage, Prowess

Mountain Lion (or Cougar) is a powerful being that excels at running, climbing, jumping, and hunting. Those who embrace Mountain Lion as their Animal are proficient at obtaining what they need through physical expertise. They go out into the world and use their somatic skills to provide for self and loved ones. Mountain Lion teaches us how to use our dynamic power of stamina to carry us far and achieve our desired results through hard work. Imbued with a natural sense of determination, those who follow Mountain Lion are able to put their persistence into action. They will stop at nothing to reach their goals and have the strength and fortitude to do so.

Mountain Lion is the epitome of lithe grace. Natural-born athletes of the forest, they can bound up to 40 ft (12 m), leap 15 ft (4.5 m) up a tree, travel long distances at 10 mph (16 kph), and reach speeds of up to 45 mph (72 kph) in a sprint. Those who hold Mountain Lion as their Animal are gifted with an agile physique and use their body with dexterity and poise.

When we reflect on the robust presence of Mountain Lion, we envision an animal with regal bearing. Feared by most mammals, this being commands respect. More closely related to domestic cats than to jungle lions, it displays its sovereignty in its dignified stature. Mountain Lion is a solitary soul. These elusive felines live near humans yet are rarely seen by them. This denotes the human propensity for enjoying time alone in the privacy of one's home and natural surroundings.

The energy of Mountain Lion is displayed in a fearless existence. Those who welcome this creature as a guide are innately courageous, with an adventurous way of being, one that does not back down. Given the choice either to boldly face danger or to retreat into safety, they prefer to risk security rather than experience boredom. When Mountain Lion appears, the wisdom offered is a lesson in how to skillfully wield the power of valiance, which results in a felt sense of true confidence.

Power

• You are skilled with the ability to work tirelessly towards your goals.

• Born with a strong physique and a natural talent for sports and movement, you have physical stamina that is admired by many. This relates to being gifted in the art of dance, as well as sports such as rock climbing and running.

• Courageous by nature, yours is the way of fearless existence.

• You carry yourself with an inborn dignity that commands respect. Those who embrace Mountain Lion energy make excellent bosses and leaders.

• You relish your privacy and will make this known to anyone who disturbs you.

Protection

• When fear emerges, connect with your source of courage. From this place of inner strength you become empowered to proceed with enthusiasm and confidence.

• When exhaustion creeps in, allow yourself time to rest and replenish your energy.

• To counterbalance boredom, activate your passion for physical activity. Go for a run, take a yoga class, or visit the climbing gym.

Wisdom

◆ You are fearless at the core of your being.

◆ Proudly adorn yourself with the crown of greatness, which is your inherent gift.

◆ Hold your head high and carry on.

Messages from Mountain Lion

When Mountain Lion emerges
reflect on your physical well-being.
Assess your current diet and self-care practices.
What can you do to re-energize your body?

Now is a good time to pick up a new
physical activity that you've been wanting to try.
Explore practices such as running,
hiking, rock climbing, yoga, dance, or tennis.

When Mountain Lion strides into your life,
evaluate the fears that are holding you back.
What are you really afraid of?

Deer

Gentleness, Generosity, Endurance

D eer is one of the most adaptable animals on earth,
native to five continents, and its powers of survival
have certainly stood the test of time. Many of the stories
about this creature revolve around a hunt, which leads
the hunter to discover new places in pursuit of Deer.
This Animal Guide embodies a desire for adventure and
a love for the outdoors. When we feel a sense of wanderlust,
Deer energy is present.

As an Animal Guide, Deer leads with gentle persuasion
into new territories. A natural wanderer, rarely following the
same path twice, this adventurous being is always willing to
explore new ways.

More than fifty different species of Deer roam the
globe. We encounter this animal regularly in the various
landscapes of fields, forests, and home gardens, as they make
themselves quite visible munching on plants and flowers.
When Deer energy becomes manifest, it signifies a time when
opportunities to embark on new quests that might be outside
our comfort zone will be presented.

Deer and humans have been in close contact for as long
as we know, with images depicted in ancient cave paintings
and petroglyphs. There was great reverence for this benevolent
being, as every part was used by indigenous peoples, for food,
fuel, clothing, and more. This partnership symbolizes the
generosity of Deer, which, as an Animal Guide, indicates an
ability to care for others with humility.

Displaying large ears, Deer possesses an acute sense
of hearing. This relates to a heightened ability to tune in to
what others are saying and act from a place of compassion.

When we are able to offer this validation, we engage Deer energy in its purest form. A keen understanding of the needs of those around us, and a powerful ability to meet those needs, are gifts that originate from this acute perception.

Power

- You have an ability to successfully take on new endeavors that require learning new skills.

- You have a penchant for travel. You may make your home in several places throughout your life.

- You possess a gift for leading others into new adventures with gentle persuasion.

- Your acute senses guide you with empathy and deep understanding.

- Generosity comes naturally to you. You are known for your kindness towards others.

- Deer energy can be seen in those whose careers ask that they explore new territories, such as travel writers, tour guides, and anthropologists.

Protection

- Proceed with caution in new endeavors. Check in with your intuition. How does it feel to enter into this new place? Trust your "gut."

- When you feel overwhelmed, take some time for inward practices such as journaling or meditation, to create a sense of safety for yourself.

- If you notice yourself feeling exhausted, take time to do something that feels nourishing. Take a walk, read a book, write in your journal.

Wisdom

• Touch your true nature. Explore and honor your wild side.

• Take adequate time to fulfill your own needs, every day.

• Balance time alone with time spent with others.

• There is more power in vulnerability than in force.

• You are your best teacher. Trust that every experience is one of learning.

• Be gentle with yourself.

Messages from Deer

Reflect on the balance of giving and receiving in your life.
Are you doing too much for others? Are your needs being met?

New adventures are on the horizon. You may soon have
the opportunity to travel to a far-off place or discover
a new area of study that will enhance your life.

When Deer appears, you can be sure that you are
entering a powerful cycle of consistent growth.
Continue to nurture projects that have been slowly evolving.

A new endeavor could be presented to you
that is outside your area of expertise.
If your senses tell you to pursue it, then do so!

When Deer emerges in your consciousness, reflect on
how you are moving through life. Where would you like to
be going and how can you get there, swiftly and easily?

Duck

Partnership, Renewal, Poise

A common bird seen regularly in parks, gardens, and backyards, Duck can be found anywhere there is water. The movements of Duck are gentle and serene, gliding along with simplicity and grace. Usually seen as part of a pair, sometimes with young following close behind, Duck symbolizes relationships grounded in love. In observing Duck's way of being, we glimpse a beautiful balance of dual energies. The wisdom conveyed is that of powerful connection with others, as well as with self. Those who embrace Duck as their Animal are robust and refined in equal measure. This energetic collaboration becomes manifest as a sense of equilibrium, which arouses a dynamic presence ready to wholeheartedly embrace partnership.

Duck females are indeed a lovely sight, yet the males are even showier and more dramatically colored. Curiously, the familiar "quack, quack" sound emanates only from the females of a few species. A vocal animal that can be heard far and wide, Duck produces a call that is more clamor than song.

Extensively hunted by humans, as well as by larger birds and mammals, Duck need to breed prolifically. The females create nests near water, in agricultural fields as well as in artificial structures in urban environments, lining the nest with grasses, leaves, and twigs. As an Animal Guide, this relates to an ability to initiate renewal through careful planning. Those who connect with Duck energy are incredibly organized and efficient when it comes to their homes in order to provide the essentials needed for their loved ones to thrive.

When we ponder Duck's habit of feeding underwater, we can relate this to an ability to cull our resources from hidden places. By obtaining nourishment from unlikely sources, we learn how to care for ourselves by trusting that we are always provided for. Those who are guided by Duck understand how to bring their needs forward through an enlightened consciousness. We become aware of new skills that will aid us in reaching our goals, or perhaps recall experiences from the past that provide us with original insights.

Power

- Your well-balanced forces of earth and spirit energies help you to exercise poise. You are firm, yet kind, intellectual, yet intuitive.

- You enjoy cultivating long-term relationships that create a sense of stability within your family.

- You possess skills associated with regeneration and renewal. Those who embrace Duck energy make wonderful homemakers and crafters.

- You maintain an ability to look within to develop greater fulfillment.

Protection

- When you feel confused about how to handle a challenging situation, turn your gaze inward to reconnect with your sense of balance.

- When loneliness creeps in, open your heart to that special someone and revel in the closeness you share.

Wisdom

* Equanimity is essential for emotional well-being.
  Be led by a balance of intuition and intellect.

* Allow your true colors to emerge, as you connect
  with the depths of your being.

* Trust in the depth of the universe to provide you
  with everything you need.

* From a place of inner power, you create tangible assets.

* Two hearts are better than one.

Messages from Duck

When Duck drifts into your life, reflect on what
you can do to develop more emotional balance.
Are you being too analytical?
Are you being overly sensitive?

Are your needs being met?
Take some time to contemplate what
it is you truly require, to feel safe and secure.
Act from your core in order
to manifest your deepest desires.

Reflect on your inner truths that are calling to be heard.
Are you giving yourself the time and
space needed to process deeper emotions?
Are you heeding the voice of intuition
and the messages in your dreams?

Bee

Productivity, Perseverance, Regeneration

Since ancient times, Bee has been considered a symbol of royalty, wisdom, mystery, fertility, and productivity. Strongly connected to the life-giving force of the sun, Bee, as an Animal Guide, teaches us how to activate our inner warmth and share our gifts with others. When we reflect on the offering of honey that bees produce, surely we can taste the sweetness in this display of giving and receiving.

The hardest-working of all insects, Bee holds special importance as a pollinator worldwide. Bee and flowers have a reciprocal relationship from which both benefit. Flowers provide Bee with the nectar and pollen needed to sustain a colony and Bee ensures the longevity of flowering plants through the process of pollination. Each hive has only one queen, with thousands of workers darting throughout the garden laboring relentlessly to produce wax, honey, and royal jelly, which fortify their species as well as ours. This fertile power relates to the energy of abundance through hard work. If Bee has emerged, you can be certain that you will be rewarded for your diligent efforts.

Bee essence is so potent that it can be hard to turn off. Those who relate to this power should be mindful to guard against overwork. Although this habit serves you well in getting things done, it can also contribute to burnout and fatigue. It's important to take time for rest, before you are forced to do so. Check in with yourself regularly. Are you doing too much? What would you like to be doing that you feel you don't have time for?

The emergence of Bee as your Animal Guide indicates an ability to persevere until goals are attained. To others, this labor appears effortless, as those guided by this Animal are endowed with a high capacity for toil. The wisdom conveyed is to remember to slow down and rest before taking up the workload again. Learning to balance our energy in this way leads to even greater success, as we become able to embrace and enjoy our rewards more fully.

Power

• You are a generous person and enjoy contributing your gifts for the greater good of all. This power also denotes an ability to help others expand their perspectives and create new awareness.

• You have a strong work ethic and are a loyal team player.

• You are incredibly organized and productive. You accomplish all your many goals through your powers of steadfast perseverance.

• Naturally gifted in the arts, you have an abundance of creative energy. Those with Bee power make excellent artists, musicians, writers, actors, and speakers.

• You have a natural ability for renewal, replenishment, and rejuvenation. When you are at your best, you embody a perfect balance of work and play.

Protection

• The symbol of the sun and its warmth are a source of buoyancy for you. To guard against lethargy, retreat into the fire of your spirit and bask in the glow of replenishment.

• When you notice a sense of fatigue from overwork, give yourself time to rest and receive the sweetness that life has to offer.

- When you feel confused and seek answers to perplexing questions, use your organizational skills to guide you towards clarity.

- Initiate collaboration with others to transform creative blocks and inspire new projects.

Wisdom

- Just because you can do it doesn't mean you have to.

- With laser-sharp focus, you accomplish all that you set out to achieve.

- You have the power within to reinvent your life.
  Allow yourself to absorb the golden light that surrounds you.

- You are capable of achieving the impossible. Dream big!

Messages from Bee

If Bee has flown into your sphere, observe your habit of overwork. What can you offer yourself right now that would contribute to inner peace?

You will soon become involved in new creative projects that require collaborative efforts and hard work. This could also symbolize a new love relationship or renewal of a current one.

Take time to slow down, rest, and enjoy all life's simple pleasures.

Fish

Sustenance, Knowledge, Cleansing

Giver of life-force energy, Fish has long been associated with sustenance. The physically nourishing properties of this amazing animal align with the emotional medicine that Fish supplies. With guidance from this Animal ally comes an effortless ability to give soul nourishment to those in need. Those who embrace Fish essence are innately connected with the fluidity of emotions and understand how to navigate psychic unrest with grace and ease.

Often touted as "brain food," Fish provides nutrients that are hard to obtain from other fare. The Celts were particularly attuned to the healing qualities offered and associated the eating of Fish with divine knowledge. Fish medicine acts as a psychic cleanser, which allows us to find solace within and continually seek enlightenment from higher sources.

Fish energy is felt as an ability to create a flow of giving and receiving. Delving into the deep waters of humanity, we experience our reliance on one another and accept the opportunities to do something for others as well. Fish has been a constant provider of sustenance to us: as an Animal Guide, it embodies a sense of humility aligned with generosity.

Of course, the multitude of different Fish species, from guppy to shark, exhibit a myriad of different traits, but the one thing they all have in common is water. This element is symbolic of dreams and inner vision. Fish guides us within, to a place of subconscious journeying, where we learn to trust our intuition as truth. As we embrace our realities in this way, we disavow illusion and continue forward with newfound understanding of what seemed complex before. We are able to view subtle signs and symbols as greater messages that are here to lead us in new directions.

Power

• You are deeply connected to your intuition and dreams
as you reflect inwardly and continually create self-awareness.

• You have a profound ability to nourish others with your
caring presence. Such is the way of spiritualists, meditators,
and religious leaders alike.

• A truly brilliant being, you are blessed with a high intellect,
grounded in divine wisdom.

• Through a deep connection with humanity, you engage
an energetic flow of giving and receiving.

Protection

• When life feels daunting and burdensome, use your
connection with water as a spiritual cleanser.

• When confusion arises, call upon your knowledge to guide
you towards understanding. From a place of clarity,
you will rise above convolution.

• If loneliness surfaces, look towards your community for
support and replenishment.

Wisdom

• Knowledge is power.

• Balance receiving with giving.

• Renew yourself in the sea of life.

• Soul nourishment is always available, as you seek
sustenance from within.

Messages from Fish

Heed the messages available from visions
and dreams. Be certain to record details
of subtle imagery that appears before you.

The arrival of Fish signifies a time
to offer your services and care to others,
from a place of selfless giving.
Trust that you have enough
to provide what is needed.

Now is a good time to assess your current
nutrition needs. Refine your diet by eliminating
unhealthy foods and cleanse your system by adding
wholesome foods and herbal supplements.

Mouse

Curiosity, Structure, Survival

Mouse exists in multitudes everywhere there are humans, but is rarely seen. We are typically alerted to its presence by the messes left behind. Reserved and curious, Mouse watches intently from a distance, inspecting what might be scavenged. Exploring our shared spaces after dark, this shy being quietly gathers resources. Those who embrace Mouse as a guide fearlessly follow what intrigues them and trust that they will obtain what is needed for survival.

Looking out through the tiny eyes of Mouse into a vast world of unknowns, we can recognize a sense of awe. The gentleness of Mouse is exhibited in the abundant food source this animal provides its predators. In an Animal Guide, we can see this as a habit of someone who serves relentlessly, and without question. Generosity is a beautiful trait that garners respect, yet when imbalanced can lead to self-sacrifice. As a teacher, Mouse leads us to our higher attribute of unconditional giving, through a balance of dynamic self-care. From the sturdy foundation of self-nourishment, we become truly empowered to meet the needs of others with an open heart.

As we observe the interplay of destruction and regeneration this animal exhibits, we recognize the duality present in Mouse energy. This tiny mammal has extraordinary powers of reproduction/productivity. Mouse mothers produce several litters per year, birthing up to fifteen babies each time. We can honor this as the bold survival of a timid species and relate it to our inborn power of a courageous soul. Conversely, this creature contributes to the ruination of food and home. It is through this dichotomy that Mouse shows us how to wield our powers with positivity in order to contribute to the development of a more evolved society. It is within these parameters that we can find ways to share our gifts for the greater good of all.

Mouse nests are artfully assembled in hidden spaces using found objects, providing comfort and safety from danger. Adept at collecting and organizing, those who hold Mouse energy possess a powerful ability to create structure amid chaos. This skill is displayed in a higher sense of order, with regard for planning and arranging.

Power

- Your natural sense of curiosity is often aroused, as you explore whatever intrigues you in each moment.

- A gentle soul who treads with care, you exercise caution before entering unknown places.

- You are inherently generous and find it easy to selflessly give to others.

- Quiet by nature, yours is the way of inner peace and serenity.

- Your high sense of order contributes to your enviable collections. Those who regard Mouse as their Animal are well organized and use this skill to joyfully display their most cherished objects.

- Mouse offers potent medicine for teachers, homemakers, and event coordinators.

Protection

- When fear arises, remain focused on the present moment and allow yourself to follow your inspirations. As you tread this path, embrace a sense of safety amid newfound excitement.

- Are you giving yourself what you need to thrive? Develop consistency with self-care practices. Carve out time each day to nourish yourself, emotionally as well as physically.

- When you feel overwhelmed by clutter, dedicate time to re-organize your space. Clean out drawers, closets, and cabinets to create a sense of peaceful order.

Wisdom

- Led by curiosity, discover joy in each moment.

- Embrace the cycles of life and create balance within.

- Give to others with a kind and open heart.

- Activate your superpower of self-care. You deserve it!

Messages from Mouse

When Mouse scurries into your life, reflect on the smaller details that surround your current affairs. Take a closer look to observe what might be missing.

In order to break monotony and procure adventure, explore new places, ideas, and interests. Book a trip to an offbeat location or take a class on an esoteric subject.

Grasshopper

Prosperity, Progress, Introspection

Since the beginning of human civilization, Grasshopper has been regarded as an almost supernatural being, revered by all those fortunate enough to cross paths with it. Grasshopper was considered a symbol of luck and prosperity throughout China, as early as the Chun Qiu period (770–476 B.C.E.). When we see this creature in the garden, flitting around and rubbing its hind legs against its wings, we observe a companion interested in the proliferation of the natural world. Grasshoppers benefit the ecosystem by keeping plant growth in balance and fertilizing the soil, and as food for predators. Those who embrace Grasshopper energy possess a wealth of resources that goes far beyond material gain.

Hopping from place to place in search of food, Grasshopper is a curious soul who appreciates examining unique perspectives. Those who exhibit Grasshopper energy are on a continual quest for knowledge, always searching for a deeper understanding of life's mysteries.

This lively insect's extraordinarily long legs symbolize forward movement. A truly fascinating animal, Grasshopper can leap as high as 20 times the length of its own body in a single bound. This physical attribute is a metaphor for the ability to look ahead with clarity of vision, in order to create change. Using this gift for forward thinking, we can assess what needs to be enacted to realize progress. Grasshopper offers valuable medicine for leaders who are working towards social improvement.

Grasshopper receives sound waves, both externally and internally, via a powerful sensory organ on its abdomen.

Through a connection of movement and breath, this insect can locate the source of subtle sound from afar. In someone with Grasshopper as their Animal, this characteristic is reflected as a heightened ability to trust our inner knowing through clairaudience. Grasshopper possesses an uncanny talent for being able to perceive the spiritual messages coded in what others say. This profound soul grants the ability to read between the lines.

Power

* Curious by nature, you always seek to extract the deeper meaning from the complexities of life. Grasshopper provides soulful companionship for those with an ability to reach metaphysical heights through the power of acute introspection—spiritualists, artists, and occultists alike.

* You are an astute listener and help others decipher the intuitive messages within themselves.

* You catalyze prosperity in all your endeavors and possess an innate quality of spiritual wealth.

* Yours is the way of progress. With extraordinary forethought, you are skilled at crafting new ideas for future advancements.

Protection

* When a sense of lack emerges, connect with your inner source of abundance. Review your resources and activate your superpower for creating emotional growth and spiritual prosperity.

* When you recognize that your usual solutions no longer work, trust in your ability to create an updated plan and carry it through with confidence.

Wisdom

* Through deep introspection, you discover the meanings of mysteries.

* Relax into your sense of personal abundance and create true prosperity.

* Trust your attunement with sound to guide you towards your ultimate source of inner knowing.

* Keep moving forward. The past is done.

Messages from Grasshopper

The arrival of Grasshopper asks you
to reflect more deeply about life.
Recognize how to make meaning of the subtle signs
and symbols that present themselves to you.

Reflect on how you perceive what others say.
From a place of stillness, open your ears more keenly,
in order to hear the subtleties that lead
to deeper awareness.

Now is a powerful time to breathe new life
into a stalled project through innovative inspirations.
What can you do differently that you haven't tried before?

When Grasshopper hops into your life
you can be certain that abundance will follow.
Watch for new opportunities and jump on the ones
that are intriguing and feel right.

Butterfly

Transformation, Grace, Beauty

B utterfly embodies the power of transformation like no other creature on the planet. Moving through four stages, the life cycle of this glorious insect illustrates the dance of fully coming into one's being. Butterfly as an Animal Guide signifies the potential for metamorphosis in all areas of life. When this graceful being flutters into your realm, you can be certain that change is on the horizon and that it will be for the better. Use its guidance to reflect on what you truly desire and embrace your deeper knowing to lead you there.

Creativity is the essence of Butterfly medicine. Whenever we follow the flight of inspiration to produce a work of art, we are led by this Animal. Through this display of dynamic self-expression we are able to show our true selves in more meaningful ways. Butterfly energy can be seen in those who are moved to work with vibrant colors, patterns, and textures, with innovation and flair. Through unbridled artistry we share our gifts, which in turn motivates others to create. And the cycle continues, ensuring that beauty will perpetually fill the garden of life.

Butterfly is an ethereal creature with extraordinary colors and movement. When we observe this being effortlessly flitting through the garden, we are deeply touched by its exquisite form. Winged beings always arrive to lead us into higher realms. Those who possess Butterfly energy are gifted at developing their inner wisdom through the course of their life and have an ability to reach many with their messages. This can be seen in those who share their spiritual ideas through writing and speaking, and relates to Butterfly as a pollinator.

Those who embrace Butterfly essence possess power through graceful activity. This relates to an acute sense of movement within the sphere of subtle energy. We see this exemplified in the way Butterfly ingests nectar by walking on flowers, keeping feet firmly grounded and wings in the air. It signifies a power of receptivity to life's gifts. People who have Butterfly as their Animal are adept at conveying ideas through body language and find it easiest to learn by doing. We observe this in types who prefer physical activity over mental process. Butterfly guides us towards our innate powers of growth through movement, in which we find the energy to catalyze change within ourselves, as we become more of who we truly are.

Power

• You are naturally creative and enjoy expressing yourself with artistry and flair.

• You possess flexibility through graceful movement. One special gift Butterfly provides is an ability to express oneself through the art form of dance.

• You have a profound ability to create deep transformation within yourself.

• Gifted in the arts, you have a talent for anything connected with music. Those who embrace Butterfly energy display their artistic gifts without inhibition and dazzle us with their brilliance.

Protection

• When you feel stuck and aspire to change your life, look within and connect with your powers of transformation to generate whatever you truly desire.

• Banish boredom! Allow yourself to get lost in creativity, in order to connect more deeply with the beauty of life.

Wisdom

- Each moment of every day is an opportunity to reinvent yourself.

- Creativity is the key to self-expression.

- Embrace all changes that come your way, trusting that they are for the best.

Messages from Butterfly

When Butterfly appears in your life, reflect on your needs. What can you release that no longer serves you? What can you embrace that will nourish you?

Take notice of how you currently express yourself. Be bold. Experiment with colors, fabrics, and textures that you would normally shy away from.

Now is an excellent time to begin a creative project or pursuit. Take lessons in painting, drawing, or dance.

When Butterfly flits into your realm, assess your current stage of emotional development. What steps do you need to take to progress to a more enlightened way of being?

Opossum

*Individuality, Introversion,
Improvisation*

T ruly one of the most unusual mammals known,
Opossum displays individuality like no other. Its more
unique traits include an ability to hang upside down by the
tail, as well as to fake death to divert humans and predators.
The animal's distinctive habits are reflected in those who
lead unconventional lives. Opossum energy can be seen in
beings who unpretentiously dress in their own style or make
quirky career choices, naturally disregarding the judgments
of others. This Animal Guide encourages us to live a life truly
desired, regardless of what others might think. Freed from
other people's expectations, we can embrace our true nature
and accept ourselves just as we are.

Playing dead when threatened, Opossum can remain
immobilized for hours and even emits a foul odor in its efforts
to be left alone. This trait symbolizes a desire for solitude
at any cost. Those who welcome Opossum as their Animal
are fundamentally introverted. The wisdom offered is to be
mindful of how we might alienate others in our desire to
procure peace. Practice asking for space in a way that allows
for kindness grounded in confidence. When we act from this
place of inner strength, we recognize that we can shed our
armor of intimidation and transform the habit of withdrawal
into the power of joining together.

We can relate Opossum's peculiar characteristic of
hanging upside down by the tail to an ability to recognize
and honor the different perspectives of others. The gift
this Animal Guide offers is especially potent medicine for
ailing relationships. From a personal standpoint, we can

tune in to our innate ability to exhibit empathy towards our friends, colleagues, and loved ones. As we become able to shift our view and see through the eyes of another, we open our hearts and thereby build a stronger foundation from which to cultivate deeper connections.

Armed with a unique skill set, Opossum is a character study in the art of improvisation. A naturally gifted actor, this eccentric being expertly feigns death or throws a staged hissy fit when intimidated or afraid. This relates to an ability to create illusion through our actions. We become adept at expressing ourselves creatively, according to the needs of each situation. We reveal only as much as we choose and emerge with a more powerful presence that contributes to developing greater expertise in all our many talents.

Power

+ You are a truly unique individual, who dances to the rhythm of your own drum.

+ You enjoy your own company over time spent with others.

+ Naturally empathetic, you have a gift for taking the perspective of another. This trait makes you a wonderful friend and partner.

+ Those who hold Opossum as their Animal are skilled in the art of acting, as well as in the fields of law and public relations.

Protection

+ When relationship challenges arise, allow yourself to take the other person's perspective. This change in awareness will help you develop stronger bonds with those close to you.

- When you feel irritated and wish to be left alone, express your needs with clarity and kindness. Expect your desires to be received with open hearts and minds. This energetic flow allows an expansion of awareness and growth, in both directions.

Wisdom

- A change in perspective, no matter how small, creates strong connections.

- Use your skills of dynamic self-expression to touch the hearts of others.

- You are a one-of-a-kind gem. Dazzle them with your many facets!

Messages from Opossum

When Opossum emerges, observe your habit of self-isolation. Reach out to friends and family to develop stronger community ties.

Assess your current relationships. Open your heart more deeply, as you receive what is being conveyed to you by others.

When you notice the presence of Opossum energy, reflect on your sense of self-acceptance. Are you able to embrace your unique gifts and express them with confidence?

Dragonfly

Artistry, Balance, Light

Q uick and dazzling, Dragonfly gracefully dips in and out
of streams, rivers, and pools. Any connection between
the elements of water and air reveals a balance of emotion
and intellect. In an Animal Guide it denotes an ability to
transform depth of emotional experience into wisdom, as we
age. This is symbolized by Dragonfly adults, which emerge
colorless, only gradually developing their final hues; many
species change color as they mature. Those who embrace
Dragonfly as their Animal are acutely aware of their fluid
emotional states, as well as their keen intellect, which creates
a sense of balance within.

Closely associated with the powers of the sun and
warmth, Dragonfly is regarded in many cultures as a bringer
of light. As the name suggests, there is a fiery quality
that surrounds Dragonfly. Reflecting the many facets of
Dragonfly energy are its ethereal colors, which shimmer
and swirl, coming alive in the light. This correlates to
sparkling charisma and connection with others in a soulful
way. Dragonfly power is expressed in those who enjoy being
in the spotlight and displaying their talents in the arts,
performance, fashion, and design. This captivating being
guides us towards our gifts of artistry, self-expression, and
beauty. When we learn how to embrace and honor these
parts of ourselves, we become more confident in sharing our
creations, which inspires others to do the same.

The habits of Dragonfly provide a metaphor for the power
to cut through illusion. Able to move each of its four wings
independently, and so fast as to be imperceptible, Dragonfly
can move straight up or down, fly backward, stop and hover,
and make hairpin turns—at full speed or in slow motion.

This uncanny skill, allowing it to dart away before reappearing elsewhere as if by magic, is symbolic of enlightenment within the mirage. As an Animal Guide, Dragonfly helps us to illuminate the truth among the shadows. When this magical being enters your life, reflect on what is not as it appears to be in order to shed light on the darkness.

When we observe Dragonfly in flight, we see a graceful creature that inspires awe. An enigmatic dancer, Dragonfly moves elegantly between water and air, absolutely uninhibited. There is much to be learned from this carefree way of being. If Dragonfly enters your life, take time to reflect on your worries and fears. Are you holding on to limiting beliefs and false ideas? Are you ready to embrace the simple pleasures that surround you? Allow this Animal to guide you to the heights of supreme authenticity and truth.

Power

+ You have an inherent gift of appreciation for beauty.

+ Your graceful presence inspires others. Those who embrace Dragonfly energy make excellent performers and artists.

+ You have a dazzling ability to cut through illusion and reflect the light in every situation.

+ You are able to embrace a healthy balance of your emotions and intellect.

+ Especially fond of the warmth of the sun, you are most effective during the summer months.

+ Dragonfly acts as a guide to those who feel passionate about caring for the world around them. This Animal Guide is especially important for homeowners, gardeners, and spiritualists.

Protection

- Be especially mindful to get enough sunlight during winter months. To counterbalance the effects of darkness, use positive affirmations, read inspiring books, and surround yourself with upbeat company.

- If you sense that things aren't what they seem, reflect on your emotional honesty with yourself. Turn on the light of deeper self-awareness to gain clarity about your emotional growth.

Wisdom

- Things are not always as they appear to be. Shine a light in the darkness to illuminate truth.

- With maturity comes true brilliance.

- Ignite your inner fire and embrace your fundamental power.

- Passionately paint the canvas of life with your unique colors.

Messages from Dragonfly

When Dragonfly darts into your life, reflect on your current sense of joy. Are you giving yourself enough time to connect with and experience the beauty of nature? Take yourself outside and frolic in gardens, parks, ponds, and rivers.

Reflect on the illusions that surround you. How are you fooling yourself or allowing yourself to be fooled by others?

Beaver

Diligence, Nurturance, Success

With a natural ability to create elaborate homes, Beaver is well equipped with unique physical attributes that can be used as building tools. With strong teeth, Beaver fells trees to use as lumber for constructing dams and lodges, and has an unusual flat tail that acts as a paddle when moving other materials, such as sticks, grass, and mud. Those who embrace Beaver have an inborn affinity for homemaking, and are skilled at developing well-organized spaces for families that are both comfortable and useful.

Beaver leads us to the places within ourselves that are boundless. With an extraordinary gift for being able to set the highest intentions for success, this industrious Animal Guide is a steadfast accomplice in helping us attain our life goals. Relentlessly working in an effortless flow is the keynote of Beaver energy. Those who look to Beaver as a guide display confidence in all their endeavors.

The industriousness that Beaver exhibits relates to the admirable human trait of hard work. Capable of taking on more than most, those who adopt the habits of this diligent soul might forget to slow down and take a break. This active animal reminds us that half of hard work is well-earned rest. It is from periods of such replenishment that we stoke our energy in order to continue our tasks with vigor. When Beaver swims into your life, pause to admire your achievements from the banks of a sunny shore.

Truly a symbol of domestic bliss, Beaver mates for life and keeps young ones nearby for the first two years, teaching them the skills they need for survival.

This mysterious rodent embodies a parental force, as seen in both the males and the females of the clan. We can view this power as a gift for being able to offer unconditional nurturance within a communal structure that supports us in activating deep familial connection.

Power

- You are passionate about creating comfortable surroundings for your family and friends. Skilled at building, you are always ready to initiate home-improvement projects.

- Beaver energy is brilliantly displayed in architects, builders, and homemakers alike.

- Your family and community are the most important structures in your life. You are nurturing by nature and care for others with a loving heart.

- You display absolute certainty in your abilities and you always achieve success in your undertakings.

- You possess tireless energy that makes others weary just watching.

Protection

- When challenges arise in your current projects, reflect on past successes to help create a more positive mindset. Envision yourself achieving your goals and allow yourself to feel the warmth and satisfaction of a job well done.

- In order to stave off loneliness, surround yourself with loved ones.

- When exhaustion overtakes you, give yourself ample time for rest. Take a nap, settle in with a good book, or simply do nothing. Emerge revived and ready to go.

Wisdom

- Can't stop. Won't stop. Don't stop.

- You are 100 percent capable of achieving your goals. Gather appropriate resources and trust that you are equipped with the tools for ultimate success.

- Find strength in your close-knit community. Lead others with love.

- Rest brings rejuvenation.

Messages from Beaver

When Beaver appears, reflect on the goals you are currently working towards. Revisit an old project and breathe new life into it. What can you continue to build on, that you've already begun?

Now is a good time to consider remodeling your home or office. Develop a plan that involves painting, furnishing, or completely transforming an unused space into an inviting one.

Have you been distant lately? Pick up the phone and reach out to loved ones. You'll be glad that you did.

The arrival of Beaver asks that you recognize your need for replenishment. Schedule time for relaxation, using a calendar if you have to.

Bear

Dependability, Safety, Introspection

The largest carnivore that lives on land, Bear is an awe-inspiring sight to behold. Even the smallest can weigh more than several adult humans, and the largest can stand 10 ft (3 m) tall. This giant reminds us that there is no need to hurry to get where we're going. It seems anyone would benefit from this wisdom, but those who hold Bear as their Animal truly have no trouble taking their sweet time to arrive at their destination. And, once they get there, the reward is tranquility.

Bear energy conveys a sense of solid dependability. This is personified in a natural ability to be steadfast and strong for those in need. These are the beings who go out of their way to create safety and nourishment, from a place of inner strength. They will give relentlessly, take time to rest and replenish, then faithfully start back up again. Such is the cycle of this nurturing soul.

When we reflect on the image of "Mama Bear," we can feel the loving support of a protective being, one who abundantly nourishes us and fills our needs. The flip side of this is the habit of domineering those who either threaten or come close to their loved ones. When Bear enters your life, reflect on your current relationships. Are you letting others live their lives? The message that Bear conveys is to relax more and trust that our loved ones are safe. This shift helps us develop a stronger capacity for giving love from a place of security, rather than from fear.

A somewhat reclusive creature, Bear semi-hibernates during the colder months. This period of sleep denotes a strong connection to the dream world. Bear energy helps us access the messages available within this mysterious realm.

From this place of elucidation, we awaken to more revealing perspectives and gain an ability to follow our will. When fully awake, Bear's hunting skills are activated, as this energized creature wades into rivers to catch a meal of fish or rips open trees to get to the honey inside. Honey represents a sweet quality of life that is indulgent as well as nourishing. Those who embrace Bear as their Animal know how to savor life and trust in the bounty that is always available.

Power

• Your peaceful presence and calm demeanor provide a strong foundation for all your endeavors and are a source of strength for others. Those who possess Bear energy find it easy to be at peace and have a natural inclination for spirituality, meditation, and counselling.

• You passionately protect those close to you and would quickly turn fierce if a loved one were in danger of being harmed.

• You have an ability to methodically nurture a project for many months, waiting for the right moment to release it to the world.

• You have a strong connection to the dream world, with an ability to embrace your higher truths.

Protection

• Bear energy offers natural protection. When someone you care about needs assistance, use your powerful presence to offer the support needed. When you feel threatened, allow yourself to display courage.

• To ensure confidence and success with creative and work projects, allow yourself extra time to prepare.

Wisdom

- Inner peace is the sanctuary of the soul.

- Allow ideas to incubate and grow. Know that your gifts will emerge when the timing is right.

- Dreams are portals to the unconscious mind.
  Embrace the signs and symbols as your inner knowing.

- Extract the sweetness of life, each day.

Messages from Bear

When Bear is awakened, reflect on how you give care to others. Are you providing your loved ones with the nourishment they need to stand on their own?

Now is a good time to evaluate your energy cycles. Be mindful to balance moments of rest with completion of chores, lest you fall into a state of laziness.

Notice your habit of saying yes.
Maybe you don't have to do it all.

Dolphin

Sensuality, Empathy, Playfulness

Dolphin inhabits every ocean on the planet, as well as some rivers. An adaptable species, they are fierce predators of other sea life, yet friendly towards humans. Throughout time, Dolphin has been observed swimming alongside boats, joyfully leaping and frolicking, purely for fun. Those who embrace this playful being as their Animal find it easy to connect with their innate source of joy and engage it often.

Dolphin has long been a symbol of the sea, reflecting humanity's reverence for its mysteries. A companion of Aphrodite, Greek goddess of love, this animal is naturally associated in our minds with all that is profound and sensual. The presence of Dolphin reminds us to enter deeply into the waters of life, with a sense of curiosity and awe. Dolphin as an Animal Guide draws us back into the primordial oceans of our being. This relates to an ability to connect with our essential creativity through self-expression. Those who recognize Dolphin as a spiritual ally embrace these mysterious parts of self, which cannot be explained, nor restrained.

One of the most intelligent creatures alive, Dolphin has an extraordinary ability to receive and transmit sounds, hearing and translating subtle frequencies through a language of chirps, squeaks, and clicks. This skill signifies a gift for picking up on the abstract messages from others and relating to people with a balance of intellect and empathy.

As a mammal, Dolphin must come up to the surface of the water to breathe. Rhythmic swimming is beautifully timed with buoyant breath, as this powerful being displays graceful strength in movement. Dolphin asks that we breathe in life deeply in order to stay afloat. Dolphin reminds us to continually connect with our vital energetic force and cultivate the nourishment that arises from within this depth.

Power

• You have a gift for communication and a renowned ability to express yourself with intelligence and compassion. Dolphin energy makes for excellent teachers, public speakers, counselors, and singers—anyone who uses their voice to convey a powerful message.

• You show much grace in all your activities and can use your body with great skill. Explore the practices of dance, yoga, martial arts, running, and other sports.

• It is easy for you to create close bonds with others. You make a wonderfully nurturing parent, partner, family member, and friend.

• You have an innate appreciation for beauty and art. Those who embody Dolphin energy make excellent artists and designers.

• You bring joy and love to all your experiences. Others are drawn to you and you have many people in your life who love and admire you.

• You are playful by nature and are always up for a rollicking good time.

Protection

• When faced with challenges in communication, you can use the power of your strong intellect and open heart to fearlessly express your voice.

- When you are met with negativity, use the power of positivity to create a loving atmosphere.

- Connect with your breath, using meditative practices, as a natural source of nourishment and inner peace.

Wisdom

- Your playful nature is a source of joy for others.

- You are never alone. Know that you have the strong support system of a caring community behind you.

- Trust your sensitive awareness to guide you through the sea of life.

- Use your voice to speak your truths.

Messages from Dolphin

When Dolphin makes its presence known,
reflect on your current communications.
Are you expressing your needs clearly?

Observe the current state of your relationships.
Are your needs and desires being met?
Are you giving to others with an open heart?

What are you taking in that doesn't serve you?
How can you bring greater nourishment to your life?

When Dolphin enters your life, you are on
the brink of giving birth to your creative endeavors.

Rabbit

Timidity, Swiftness, Rebirth

R abbit has a reputation as a timid creature of yards, gardens, and fields and can be seen munching on any green thing in its path. When threatened, it exercises caution, and speedily runs for cover in the face of danger—and anything from a human passerby to a howling coyote can signify danger to this vulnerable being. Worldwide, Rabbit is one of the most abundant food sources for larger animals. In the Animal Guide, this is reflected in a trait of giving to others from the core of being. Those who identify with Rabbit energy enjoy tending to the needs of loved ones yet need to stay mindful that they are putting their own needs on the back burner while doing so.

Those who embrace Rabbit as their Animal enjoy going about their business quietly, and sidestep confrontation at all costs. This mirrors the animal's ability to go from complete stillness to high-speed escape in a matter of seconds. Rabbit's inherent knack for self-protection is personified in those who are attracted to spiritual practices. Feeling completely at ease with solitude and introspection, Rabbit reminds us that we can empower ourselves from a foundation of quiet inner strength.

Rabbit is highly sensitive and can detect food sources as well as threats from afar. This animal guide gives the gift of a natural ability to perceive what will transpire. Offering protection from peril, this courageous soul leads us towards safety by quickly ushering us out of harm's way. With lightning speed, this Animal Guide teaches us how to improve a difficult situation, swiftly and with ease. Rabbit energy acts as a catalyst for transformation in the face of challenges.

We might expect a species continually at the mercy of predators to be annihilated, yet Rabbit regenerates at a rapid rate. Females become pregnant from a young age and bear litters of six or so, several times a year. As we reflect on the contrast between life and death that is apparent in this display, we can see the natural balance that Rabbit symbolizes. For this reason, cultures worldwide honor Rabbit as sacred. In Greek mythology, Rabbit is connected to Aphrodite, goddess of love. Indigenous tribes of Mexico and Central America regard Rabbit as a symbol of fertility. The essence of procreation, this being carries the seeds of all future generations.

Power

- You have a powerful ability to create quickly and accomplish much, as you are skilled in fully using your dynamic bursts of energy.

- You are quick-witted and quick to act. An ability to think on your feet gets you out of sticky situations fast.

- You are a kind-hearted being. Your generosity knows no bounds, as you enjoy giving to others.

- You have a natural gift for working with plants, flowers, and food. Those who possess Rabbit energy make wonderful gardeners and cooks.

Protection

- When you feel depleted by caring for others, renew your energy by taking time for yourself in a nourishing environment. Go for a walk in the woods or tend the garden in order to replenish yourself.

- As a guardian, Rabbit can transform feelings of nervousness, timidity, and fear into courage, strength, and confidence. By embracing your inner strength you become able to feel an unshakable sense of safety and security.

Wisdom

- Self-love is the foundation of all love.

- Treat yourself as well as you treat others.

- Nature heals. Touch the flowers and play in the garden, each day.

Messages from Rabbit

When Rabbit hops into your life,
reflect on your current state of self-care.
In what ways can you give yourself the
same level of care that you afford others?

A birth of some sort is on the horizon.
This could signify the culmination of a project,
completion of a work of art, or the actual birth
of a child for yourself or someone close to you.

Eagle

Focus, Excellence, Perception

From high up on a perch, Eagle surveys the surroundings with extraordinarily sharp focus. Those who hold Eagle as their Animal possess incredible clarity of perception, which contributes to their hard-earned success. They develop a complex plan and work within this blueprint to achieve their highest aim. Continually soaring to new heights, Eagle energy is the epitome of magnificence. With a wingspan of greater than 7 feet (2 m), this exalted bird has a powerful presence. This mighty being teaches us to reach for what we might think is beyond our limits in order to achieve true greatness.

Most cultures regard Eagle as a sovereign guardian, presiding over the land. Ancient Roman, German, and French armies all marched under the sign of Eagle as an icon of strength and fortitude. The Aztecs believed Eagle was the force that moved the sun in its passage across the sky and all indigenous North American tribes embraced Eagle as a sacred animal that could approach the creator most nearly. This symbolizes an ability to connect with potent sources of enhanced vision and perception. From this place of scrutiny, truths emerge that lead us to our deepest wisdom.

As well as being able to soar, Eagle can swoop gracefully to clasp prey in its talons. Observing this massive creature acting with such agility inspires us to take hold of our destiny and attain whatever provides us with nourishment. As an Animal Guide, Eagle teaches us how to engage life with our feet firmly planted on the earth and our aspirations lifted towards the heavens. From this dizzying peak, we can attain our goals and fulfill our greatest ambitions.

We might think of Eagle as a solitary being, yet its powers of partnership are well developed. Mating for life symbolizes strength in family bonding and is reflected in those who regard Eagle as a teacher. When we observe the majestic mating rituals performed by this mystical bird, we can relate this to a dynamic sexual energy that carries lovers into the sphere of eternal commitment. This is the dance of soulmates who are willing to explore the zenith of partnership.

Power

• You have a dynamic physical presence that attracts others through your sensual gifts.

• You know how to build long-term relationships and are loyal to those you love.

• You possess a well-balanced spiritual energy, displayed in divine wisdom.

• Those who embrace Eagle energy do well in careers that require intense focus, such as teaching, science, and community leadership.

Protection

• When you feel stuck in over-intellectualization, allow yourself to connect with your higher source of wisdom. Reflect on your experiences from a place of feeling rather than from mind.

• When you are discouraged and unable to move forward to achieve your goals, envision yourself in your most powerful form, adorned with a crown of greatness. Know that you are perfectly capable of realizing anything that you set your mind to.

Wisdom

• Dare to be great.

• Fearlessly soar to new heights, while keeping yourself grounded in the supportive energy of the earth.

• Keep your eye on the prize and don't lose sight of what truly matters.

• True wisdom comes from experience, not intellect.

Messages from Eagle

When Eagle lands in your sphere,
reflect on how you can expand your perspective.
What keeps you playing for small stakes?
Allow your excellence to emerge without restraint.

Now is a good time to explore new spiritual customs.
Practice meditation, read self-help books,
or develop your skills in the metaphysical arts.

The arrival of Eagle signifies a new relationship
on the horizon or perhaps reaching new peaks
in a current partnership.

Turtle

Ancient Wisdom, Longevity, Security

One of the most ancient creatures on the planet, Turtle has been long revered as a venerable symbol of earth energy, which relates to all that is sacred. When we reflect on the wisdom this Animal Guide holds, we can connect deeply with our primal roots of ancestral insight. Through an innate sense of safety and security, we can delve deeper into the seas of life and cull the nurturance that is there to hold us and heal us. At the most profound level, Turtle energy can be felt at the core of humanity. It is within this flow that we can call upon this animal to guard us and lead us towards our primeval way of being.

As we embrace Turtle as a guide, we sense a calm, steady presence that embodies the grace of old age. This being has a depth of inner knowledge and a gift for steadfast patience, which makes for flexibility in all endeavors. We learn the secrets of adaptability from this creature's ability to live both on land and in water. When we discover how to flow through life in this way, we create an endurance that supports us to engage in a long, peaceful existence. A keynote of Turtle energy is longevity. To find a connection with Turtle as an Animal Guide is to discover our powers of fortitude and inner strength. Turtle bends but is not broken. Using this stamina we are able to engage healthy cycles of life, which lead to long-lasting well-being.

Turtle possesses a highly developed sense of smell, as well as being able to keenly feel vibrations through the earth and water. Vision is their strongest sense, as they can see in color, at night, and underwater. When this animal appears in your life, it signifies an innate capacity for attunement through sharp powers of perception. Those who regard Turtle as their Animal are gifted with a powerful ability to empathize with others. You may notice this as a heightened sensitivity to the energies that surround you. By using your powers of inner strength, you can trust that you are protected as you connect with and lend support to others.

Power

* You embody a peaceful presence with an ability to stay grounded in the moment. Your way is one of inner strength.

* Deeply in tune with earth's ancient energies, you are wise beyond your years. You possess a strong connection to ancestral wisdom, which supports your skills for working with plants, animals, and gems.

* You are gifted with heightened sensory perception, which allows you to easily exercise empathy for others.

* Your dwelling is the center of your life. You create a safe and loving space and enjoy working from your home.

* You possess the gift of flexibility. You are able to easily embrace the dualities of groundedness and fluidity.

Protection

* When you feel threatened, you can create a sense of security by retreating within. From this place of inner strength you will emerge fearless.

* If you are feeling frayed by the fast pace around you, pause and remind yourself to slow down and take it easy.

* Those who regard Turtle as their Animal need ample time alone for reflection through meditation and journaling.

Wisdom

• Slow and steady wins the race. Perseverance and careful planning lead to long-term success.

• Our time on earth is brief, yet our ancient wisdom lives on and spans generations to come.

• Trust that the earth provides all that you need. Give thanks for this soulful nourishment that feeds body, mind, spirit, and soul.

• Seek the ancient wisdom within yourself.

Messages from Turtle

Is life moving too fast? When Turtle emerges,
this is a reminder to allow yourself time for self-care.

As a token of ancient earth energy, the presence
of Turtle in your life relates to profound messages from
the spirit world. Pay close attention to signs, symbols,
and dreams, as you reflect deeply within.

Notice how you are using your senses.
Are you tuned in to your inner knowing?
What are your senses trying to tell you?

A visit from Turtle signifies a need to connect more
deeply with the earth. Act on this by taking a hike,
swimming in rivers, and cultivating gardens.

Skunk

Boundaries, Vulnerability, Peacefulness

When we observe Skunk, oddly striped and equipped with predator repellent, we witness a powerful being armed with natural fortitude to guard against trouble. Vintage medical texts report the use of odiferous Skunk spray as a cure for lung maladies. A distinctive character, Skunk is one of the few mammals that come furnished with this peculiar safeguard against predators. As an Animal Guide this symbolizes an innate ability to cull unusual resources to create greater health and well-being. Those who regard Skunk as a guide possess a wide array of esoteric skills, which makes for excellent holistic healers and spiritual leaders.

The essence of Skunk is that of boundaries. When we reflect more deeply on the trait of spraying an acrid oil up to 15 ft (5 m) to keep others at a distance, we can relate this to a habit of extreme introversion. Both the pungent odor emitted and the bold striped coat are powerful tools to ward off other beings—even the most brazen predators will back away in the face of Skunk. This symbolizes an ability to create clear guidelines and command respect from others. Skunk as an Animal Guide empowers us to be firm and stand tall. We learn how to stay true to ourselves, while alerting others to our convictions from afar.

Those who hold Skunk as their Animal prefer to be left alone and, if disturbed, will snap. On a soul level, we may see this as profound vulnerability, with a fear of creating healthy connections with others. The wisdom Skunk offers is to learn how to open our hearts, build trust, and embrace the benefits of loving partnerships.

As guarded as Skunk is, a natural quality of serenity surrounds this creature. All the traits mentioned previously characterize an animal that enjoys a peaceful existence. Skunk uses its natural repellent only when other warnings fail. Thriving in quiet places alone at night, this solitary being performs an intricate dance in an effort to procure peace and when not understood will use its spray as a last resort. With its placid presence this Animal Guide is a special guardian to those who choose reclusive lifestyles hidden away from social norms, such as nuns, monks, priests, and spiritualists.

Power

- You are a skilled healer who uses unconventional methods to create well-being. Those who embrace Skunk energy make excellent herbalists, energy healers, and empaths.

- You have strong boundaries and stand tall in your convictions.

- You possess a peaceful presence. A natural-born introvert, you prefer time spent alone.

Protection

- Skunk provides protection using natural resources. In order to create greater health and well-being, use your vast storehouse of healing techniques and medicines.

- When vulnerability arises, use guided visualizations and crystals that focus on creating a sense of safety within.

- When working with others, exercise your authority firmly, yet gently. Your ideas will be better received if they are delivered with kindness.

Wisdom

- Vulnerability is a strength when grounded in an open heart.

- Soften your boundaries to allow for deeper connections. Know that you are safe.

- You embody inner peace and serenity. Allow others to get close enough to enjoy the essence of tranquility that you emit.

Messages from Skunk

When Skunk emerges in your life,
assess your current state of health.
Align yourself with practices that contribute
to emotional and physical well-being.
Refine your diet, practice meditation,
and be consistent with your exercise routine.

Now is a good time to reflect on
how you communicate your ideas and inspirations.
Do you offend others when you convey your message?
How might you express yourself with more softness?

Observe your habit of self-isolation.
Challenge yourself by joining a weekly exercise class
or book club in order to connect with others.

Squirrel

Energy, Organization, Abundance

The industrious energy of Squirrel can be felt simply by observing this creature at work. Agile and acrobatic, climbing trees, fences, and bird feeders, Squirrel amasses and hoards nuts, seeds, berries, and flowers year-round, keeping stashes hidden in various locations throughout its territory. Gathering and organizing is the game, as this small animal amasses what is needed for survival. Squirrel signifies an ability to manage life through the ever-changing cycles of the year and to dance within this rhythm.

Those who embrace Squirrel as their Animal are hard-working, highly capable beings who embody the energy of doing. Moving swiftly yet carefully, with deft skill and a nimble body, defines this power of productivity. Scurrying about, Squirrel appears as a purposeful creature, when actually much of its behavior is territorial. Seemingly jocular antics are signals to predators to stay away. We often hear loud chirping as a warning in the presence of owls, snakes, and foxes.

Skilled at gathering and sorting, those who relate to Squirrel energy often have enviable collections of precious objects. With a natural gift for organization, they have a practical ability to store items for future use. We can look towards Squirrel's gift for collecting as a reminder to use our resources in order to take care of our surroundings.

When we reflect on the habit of food hoarding displayed by Squirrel, we can relate this to the human fear of not having enough. The creation of abundance through gathering illustrates beautifully that there is indeed plenty to go around. Those who embrace Squirrel as their Animal can recognize when they feel a sense of lack and practice generosity, to create balance.

Power

• You are the epitome of energy. A high-functioning individual who enjoys working hard, you are at your best when you create balance by taking time for rest and renewal.

• You are skilled at planning ahead and you are always prepared for future events. Those who possess Squirrel energy make excellent event coordinators and organization leaders.

• You have a natural talent for getting things done. Once you put your mind to it, there's no stopping you.

• Squirrel skills contribute to prowess in antiques dealing, statistics research, and collecting of every sort.

Protection

• Relax! When stress arises, give yourself time to unwind. Engage regularly in restorative practices, such as yoga and meditation.

• With Squirrel as a guardian, you can prepare yourself in the face of emergencies. To create a sense of safety, gather supplies in advance and make ready tools for future use.

Wisdom

• Balance your energy between work and play. To ensure top performance, allow yourself time to rest and rejuvenate.

• Embrace Squirrel energy as a guide to creating more order in your life and accepting more peace as a result.

• Brief moments of relaxation bring lasting renewal.

• You have everything you need, and more.

Messages from Squirrel

When Squirrel makes an appearance,
be careful of fatigue and burnout from overwork.
Give yourself extra time to relax
and restore your inner resources.

You are entering a phase of heightened activity.
Observe how you expend your energy
to achieve the most productive outcomes.

Reflect on your current state of need.
Are you taking too much
when others don't have enough?
Practice giving in order to establish
a sense of abundance.

When Squirrel makes its presence known,
view what needs to be cleared out,
either in your physical space or in your
emotional sphere. Is the clutter in your home
asking to be sorted? Are you holding in feelings
that wish to be expressed?

Snake

Transcendence, Duality, Healing

O ne of the most controversial animals on the planet,
Snake has long been a prominent symbol of duality,
featuring in myriad stories of good and evil. Some indigenous
cultures regarded this mysterious creature as a harbinger of
transformation. Ancient Greek civilizations held Snake as
symbolic of medicine and it is still the emblem of healers and
physicians today. In Hindu mythology, Lord Vishnu is shown
with Ananta, the creature with infinite coils that represents
the process of creation. These are all admirable traits, and
yet there is much lore dealing with Snake's dark power over
humans. The wisdom offered by this Animal Guide is to
mindfully observe the dichotomies within ourselves in order
to activate empowered change. When we are able to accept
and embrace our polarities as unique parts of our whole
experience, we become truly able to transcend our challenges.

A unique animal, Snake exhibits a mesmerizing presence
that draws us in, with caution. Fascinating, if not somewhat
fearsome, this reptile can shed its skin, symbolizing an
impressive power of transformation. Snake guides us within
and asks that we recognize what no longer serves us, and
release any excess into the universe. What remains is renewal,
catalyzing profound physical and emotional health.

When we reflect on the habits of this slithering soul,
we view a being gifted with phenomenal flexibility but
grounded in the energy of the earth. Snake teaches us how
to attain depth of being through empowerment of our divine
physical form. Those who embrace Snake as their Animal
possess a profound relationship to their bodies, through
spiritual practices. Such is the way of yoga devotees, qi gong
practitioners, and dancers alike.

With a flickering, forked tongue Snake smells whatever it will consume. Being able to locate nourishment in this way symbolizes a character that is attuned to the subtle nuances of life and absorbs it all with keen perception. Snake encourages us to trust our inner wisdom, which helps us to become aware of our highest sources of spiritual sustenance.

Power

• You are an emotionally honest person, able to reflect inwardly about your shortcomings in order to enact positive change.

• Gifted in the healing arts, you delve deeply into your abundant resources to catalyze health and well-being, for yourself as well as for others. Snake provides potent medicine for healers, herbalists, and alchemists.

• Agility is your strength, as is displayed in your graceful physical presence.

• You are highly attuned to subtle energy and find it easy to follow the scent towards deep sources of wisdom.

Protection

• There are two sides to every story. When you are stuck and feel unable to move beyond a current challenge, reflect on the duality which is present. By being able to take a different perspective, you create spiritual and emotional growth.

• When you or a loved one is suffering, connect with your innate healing powers. Know that you are instinctively equipped to manage the health and emotional difficulties that arise.

Wisdom

- Transcend your challenges, as you embrace all your experiences as opportunities for growth.

- From out of the darkness, light will emerge.

- Trust that your senses will never lead you astray.

- What do you need in order to heal?

Messages from Snake

When Snake slithers into your path, reflect on what you are currently holding onto that no longer serves you. What can you release, right now?

Now is an excellent time to assess your health and create positive lifestyle changes. Explore a healthier diet, get a massage, or adopt new mindfulness techniques.

The arrival of Snake signifies a need for inner reflection in order to discover your ultimate sources of nourishment.

Blue Jay

Self-Expression, Hope, Power

One of the first signs of spring in North America, the arrival of Blue Jay signifies the emergence of new life. As the days grow longer, the songs from the trees call us outside into the warmth and light. After the darkness of winter, a sense of hope is ignited and catalyzes our growth within. Those who recognize Blue Jay as their Animal continually remind us that the brilliant sun always rises, beyond the shadows of night. With this guidance, we become enlivened to face a new day with the gift of hope in our hearts.

Winged wise ones always point us in the direction of our higher truths. Blue Jay is no exception. Soaring from tree to tree, this magnificent bird flaunts an ethereal shade of blue, which signifies both the sea and the sky. Blue Jay energy connects us to the divine essences of earth and spirit. As we embrace this sense of empowerment we become able to convey our deeper wisdom.

A crest of feathers behind Blue Jay's neck is an indicator of what this animal is experiencing. Whether raised, fluffy, or flat, it denotes a particular emotional state. When we reflect on this habit, we see a being who expresses its emotions through body language. Blue Jay teaches us how to connect with our inner state on a deeper level and let others know how we are feeling from a place of self-possession.

Often regarded as a forceful creature, Blue Jay symbolizes a powerful presence. Those who hold this feathered friend as their Animal find wisdom in learning how to wield their power with grace, rather than force. Confident souls such as these benefit from honing their skills over time.

Exuberance early in life can be recognized and developed into passion for a greater purpose or cause that knows no bounds. As we grow and mature, we can use our individual emphatic nature to work towards the empowerment of larger communities, to help catalyze universal change.

Power

- You have a buoyant and uplifting spirit, which often carries you into higher states of consciousness.

- Skilled in the art of language, you captivate others when you speak. Your wisdom is a conduit for higher ideals. Blue Jay makes excellent medicine for anyone whose work involves reaching others through the spoken and written word.

- You possess a dynamic ability to express yourself through physical movement.

- Provocative and outspoken, your way of being is courageous. Be mindful not to get caught in overzealous assertions.

Protection

- When you sense negativity in your atmosphere, seek to connect with your gift of inner hope. Take some time to recalibrate the energy that surrounds you by indulging in positive activities. Watch the sunset, call a friend who lifts your heart, or simply pause to smell the flowers.

- Blue Jay energy helps us to stand up for our beliefs from a place of courage. When you feel you need to convey your message boldly and loudly, reflect inwardly and strengthen your ability to express yourself calmly and clearly.

Wisdom

♦ The world is how you see it. Choose hope and know that positivity shines on in those who expect it.

♦ Sing your song of wisdom from the highest branch of the tallest tree.

♦ Your body is a vibrant instrument of self-expression.

♦ Gentle actions create powerful results.

Messages from Blue Jay

When Blue Jay lands in your path,
reflect on how you currently view the world.
Notice how often negative thoughts cloud your mind.
Allow yourself to rest in the peacefulness of positivity.

Now is a good time to pause and assess how you
communicate with others. Are you using your gift of
melodious speech to convey your views with kindness?

You are entering a powerful phase of creativity.
Approach life with newfound artistry
by connecting with your gift of fearless flair.

Spider

Creativity, Complexity, Reverence

With tens of thousands of species throughout the world, Spider is one of the more common creatures on the planet. As most are venomous, this misunderstood being has a reputation for being fearsome, although rarely harmful to humans. Maybe what lends substance to this intriguing reputation is the circuitous dance it displays when constructing an elaborate web out of naturally produced silk. Spider manufactures different silks to cope with various challenges, such as trapping prey, traveling, protecting egg sacs, and creating shelter. Or perhaps it's the fact of having many eyes (usually eight) that gives this animal an eerie presence. This Animal Guide activates our deep inner vision and expands our ability to see things from various perspectives.

The essence of Spider is that of ancient wisdom. The sacred geometry displayed in the two sections of Spider's body forms a figure eight. We can relate this to the infinity symbol—all that is included in the past, with a bridge towards the future. Indigenous North American tribes held Spider as supreme "grandmother wisdom," embodying the highest feminine values of love, nurturance, and insight. Keeper of the truths of humanity, deeply connected to the earth, Spider is here to teach us reverence for all our experiences, so that we may weave together strong resources for future challenges.

We can see deep complexity displayed in the juxtaposition of the life cycle of Spider, as females assiduously protect their egg sacs, while the males generally die after mating. This is symbolic of the polarity between birth and death. As an Animal Guide, we can view this as a lesson in developing greater balance in our relationships and undertakings.

From a place of equilibrium, we find stability within the complexities of life.

When we observe the intricate patterns effortlessly created by this tiny creature, we witness a highly skilled artist at work. A phenomenal structure built entirely of natural silk is a beautiful metaphor for the ability to design and construct from a place of uninhibited creativity, with the use of organic resources. Spider energy is powerful medicine for anyone who leads their life with artistry and grace. An innate ability to express oneself boldly through a passionate partnership with art is a glorious gift from this Animal Guide. Those who embrace Spider energy make excellent artists, weavers, and writers.

Power

+ You are highly creative by nature, with an ability to construct intricate objects. A discerning eye, coupled with artistic flair, makes for gifted artists, architects, builders, and homemakers.

+ You possess an innate skill for deep inner vision, which you often use to lead others into greater awareness.

+ An old soul, you are profoundly in touch with the mysteries of life.

+ Intense and complex, you are regarded as mysterious by others. You are well served by striving for balance in your relationships.

Protection

* Engage your powers of creativity to transform boredom into excitement. Register for an art class in an unexplored genre or dust off your sketch pad and trek to an inspirational location.

* When confusion arises, connect with your ancient roots of inner knowing to guide you to clarity and truth.

Wisdom

* Embrace your dynamic essence of self-expression. Allow your artistry to flow freely and reach the hearts of others.

* You hold the truths of all generations before you and the potential for all generations to come.

* Through balance you display true power.

Messages from Spider

When Spider makes its presence known, reflect on your roots. Explore your family origins to discover wisdom that will guide you into the future.

Observe how you currently behave in your relationships. Are you judging others harshly? Are you over-protecting those you love? Practice developing balance by releasing expectations and trusting in the universe.

When Spider enters your life consider redecorating or remodeling your space. Now is the perfect time to create an artistic vision for your home.

Raccoon

Agility, Authenticity, Earth

Regarded as pests that ransack trash cans in search of food, Raccoon is one of the most prolific and fascinating creatures of urban legend. With supreme dexterity this clever being searches and pillages until it gathers what it wants, be it human refuse or pond fish. When we observe Raccoon's nimble fingers we can relate this trait to an enhanced ability to use our hands skillfully in our daily work. From a place of generosity, we can offer our gifts to others as a source of nourishment.

A nocturnal creature that walks with feet firmly on the ground yet feels at home in the water, Raccoon has a prominent connection to our divine life-force energy. Those who embrace Raccoon as a guide are comfortable when exposed to the elements. With an extraordinary ability to join with nature and cherish the planet, Raccoon as an Animal Guide leads us to our rightful place as stewards of the earth. As we become more able to exercise our power within this sacred partnership, we can step up and effectively work towards the greater good of all.

The most characteristic feature of this marvelous creature is its facial markings. Known as a "bandit" because of its unique masked face, as well as its habit of stealing food, this enigmatic animal helps us to look within to discover how we might abandon pretense and allow our authentic selves to emerge. When Raccoon appears, we are being asked to reflect on our true nature and look for clues to help us understand who we really are, at the core of our being. Raccoon medicine encourages us to develop a more loving view of ourselves and to wholeheartedly embrace all our distinctive parts, without worrying about keeping up appearances.

A remarkably agile being, Raccoon climbs with strength and grace. Fearless in ascending trees of any height, it denotes a keen power of reaching for higher truths. Raccoon energy encourages the exploration of consciousness from a place of elevated vision. This adept creature can also easily descend a tree, head first, which is symbolic of a link between the essences of heaven and earth. From a place of heightened spirit, grounded in depth of soul, Raccoon teaches us to implement mindfulness in order to develop an empowered way of being. This Animal Guide offers useful medicine for those who practice meditation and shamanic journeying.

Power

- You are adept at using your hands, for labor as well as for enjoyment. Those who hold Raccoon as their Animal make excellent crafters, bakers, carpenters, and massage therapists.

- You possess an enlightened consciousness, as you are deeply aware of the connection between the essences of heaven and earth.

- Raccoon energy is alive in your genuine reverence and care for the planet.

- You strive to carry yourself with authenticity, as you continually develop new awareness of your true way of being.

Protection

- When you feel disheartened about the fate of the planet, call upon others to contribute their skills to develop an empowered future for the earth. Know that you possess the gifts to effectively create change.

- Do you put on a façade for fear of not being accepted? To develop more confidence, practice expressing yourself as you would truly like to do. Allow yourself to voice something that you would normally keep inside or do something that you only dream of doing.

Wisdom

- Know that your handiwork deeply touches the hearts of others.

- When you honor the earth as sacred, you create regeneration of the planet.

- Bravely be you. Without fear. Without pretense.

- Practice being vulnerable by staying true to yourself.

Messages from Raccoon

When Raccoon enters your life,
reflect on your current commitment to the earth.
Assess how you interact with the natural world
around you. Join with people and organizations who
are working to create positive change.

The arrival of Raccoon asks that you consider
how you portray yourself to the outside world.
Are you allowing your authentic self to emerge?

Dog
Loyalty, Protection, Fun

O ur intrinsic connection with Dog is valued by most cultures worldwide. When we think of Dog, renowned as "human's best friend," we think of camaraderie. Of all the domestic animals with whom we share a natural affinity, Dog is the most universally cherished. The companionship provided by this faithful guardian has been a foundational element of our existence for the past 25,000 years. As an Animal Guide, Dog relates to an ability to create deep relationships with others, grounded in abiding loyalty. Those who possess this quality cultivate long-lasting friendships through constancy and care.

Those who have Dog as a pet are keenly aware of its protective qualities and how our lives are shaped by this security. Most of us have had the direct experience of emotional safety in the company of our stalwart companions. In unspoken ways, we feel the care offered, through loving eyes and soft sighs. We trust this reliable being to guard our homes and families, as well as our hearts. Stories are often told of the joys elicited through a connection with a newly adopted pet. Those who embrace Dog as their Animal have a special ability to extend emotional support to others. Through a sense of safety and warmth, a lasting bond is created.

Originally domesticated from wolves, Dog displays heightened sensory perceptions akin to those of its wild ancestors. This trait symbolizes an innate ability to understand what others are feeling. Those who possess Dog energy are natural-born detectives who can sniff out the root of the problem and aid others in creating deeper awareness. Dog shares the wisdom of being able to listen closely.

By trusting our intuitive faculties, we can tune in to the subtler messages and bring a newfound understanding into the light.

Another lively gift this Animal Guide shares is that of playful joy. As we observe pups frolicking and darting about, their free-flowing enthusiasm inspires us to join in. Whether on an intentional play-date at the dog park or taken by surprise in the middle of the afternoon, we experience the pure pleasure in rolling around with these amusing playmates. We feel a sense of jubilation in our hearts as we connect with our animal allies, just for fun. This indicates an ability to regard amusement as essential. Those who live life to the fullest, and hold play in equal balance with work, create a sense of delight in all they do.

Power

- You are a steadfast friend. It is easy for you to open your heart to your closest pals, as you go out of your way for those you love.

- You cherish time spent in amusement and are often the one who assembles a group to partake in fun-filled events.

- You possess an extraordinary gift for being able to innately understand what others are feeling and offer steadfast support in challenging times. Dog energy makes for excellent counselors, activists, and companions.

Protection

- When you find it difficult to manage emotional challenges, remember that you have a close circle of friends who are always available to you for love and support. Reach out to those whom you implicitly trust.

- Has life become boring? Connect with your power of playful joy.

- Gather friends together and call for a game night or a soccer afternoon, just for fun.

Wisdom

- Know that you are never alone. Your circle of support is everlasting.

- Rely on your keen senses to guide you in understanding the greater meaning in what others convey.

- Consistent time for play keeps the mind supple, the heart young, and the soul nourished.

Messages from Dog

When Dog appears, reflect on those whom you rely on for emotional support, as well as on how you offer care to others. Is your circle of friends strong? How can you create deeper connections?

Observe how you currently engage playful joy in your life. Create time to revel completely and allow your soul to be nourished by this essential merriment.

Crow

Vocalization, Empowerment,
Socialization

The most prominent signifier of Crow is the familiar "caw" that echoes throughout urban environments, as this expressive animal is not shy about making its presence known. We've all heard the clamor, which changes based on the message being conveyed. The deeper wisdom symbolized by Crow is that of being able to raise our voices with certainty and reach others through clarity of vision. Those who hold Crow as their Animal possess a natural ability to catch the attention of others, while speaking up about their beliefs, philosophies, and dreams. Through this inspired vocalization, we become truly powerful in our efforts to catalyze positive social change.

As is displayed in the dense flocks that gather along highways or in open fields at dusk, Crow energy represents the roots of socialization. Some will fly as far as 50 miles (80 km) to join in the revelry. We can relate this phenomenon to a deep desire for interaction through community connection. Crow encourages us to join wholeheartedly with others and to thrive within this amiable bond.

A keen intellect makes Crow distinct from other birds. This astute creature is known to outsmart other animals. Constructing nests high up in the tops of trees in order to scrutinize the land below, Crow scans and surveys with a watchful eye, keeping a lookout for potential dangers. These are the guardians of the neighborhood, who observantly prepare for and give warning of possible challenges. The lesson offered is to become proficient in our skills for managing external difficulties in order to create a feeling of safety within. From this place of inner strength, Crow guides us to our highest wisdom and reveals the courage to proceed further in our efforts for the greater good of all.

When we observe the rich blue-black of Crow's feathers, we view a being associated with the energy of darkness. Such depth of color symbolizes a gift for elucidating the dream world and the mysterious messages within that space. As we gaze into our subconscious experience, we become more familiar with the inner truths that are hidden in daylight shadows. Crow teaches us to connect with these deeper meanings and to cull the wisdom that leads us to our higher knowing. With this elevated awareness comes the ability to forge ahead with clarity and confidence.

Power

* You possess a high intellect, which serves you well in managing challenges. From this skillful perch, you offer steadfast protection.

* With a stellar gift for vocalizing your views with lucidity and boldness, you reach the ears of others, far and wide. Crow provides potent medicine for public speakers, performers, and social activists.

* A strong community is vitally important to your emotional well-being and is a potent source of your power.

* You have an innate ability to understand and interpret dream symbolism and messages from the unconscious mind.

Protection

* When you feel isolated or lonely, reach out to your greater community of family, friends, and colleagues. Know that the support of others is always available to you.

- A natural-born guardian, you are easily able to offer protection to self and others, from a place of thoughtful intelligence.

- When uncertainty surfaces, reflect on your inner knowing and practice connecting with your innate power of intuition. Trust that your truth is within.

Wisdom

- Find your voice and don't be afraid to use it.

- Participation with others creates a strong foundation for all your endeavors.

- In order to realize your deepest truths, look for messages in the unknown.

- Hold your vision strongly. Trust your inner wisdom. Proceed with empowerment.

Messages from Crow

When Crow lands in your realm, observe how you currently honor your community connections. Is there a new organization or club that you would like to join?

The arrival of Crow denotes the development of your voice. Now is a powerful time to practice speaking your truth. Explore singing, spoken-word poetry, or organizations that align with your beliefs.

When Crow flies into your space, reflect on the deeper meanings of dreams. Trust your intuition to guide you.

Lizard

Sensitivity, Confidence, Reflection

The image of lazy Lizard, lounging in the sun, is one we all recognize. On long summer days, blending in with the landscape, this ancient being can be seen happily immobilized in midday warmth. When we reflect on the energy of the sun, we can see the ways in which this powerful force symbolically imbues those who hold Lizard as their Animal with a sense of vitality and confidence.

We're usually unaware of this incognito animal until we hear a scurrying sound and see a scaly tail quickly dart away. Lizard energy denotes a stealthy ability to go unnoticed, while carefully surveying and considering our next move. When this curious creature "plays dead," it symbolizes an ability to fend off the attention of others by feigning complete ignorance. Lizard medicine reminds us to actively take time for inner reflection before making important decisions or plans, and to proceed with caution in partnerships. When we learn to go inward, trusting our power of heightened awareness, we become unafraid and able to proceed with certainty on our path.

Lizard energy encapsulates a deep sensitivity. A mystical aura surrounds this Animal Guide, a fragile being that seems barely there. An exceptional ability to detect the slightest movements of insects through the vibrations of the earth denotes the gift of psychic awareness. With extraordinary powers of perception, Lizard has been held in high regard by many ancient cultures. To Egyptians, the presence of this reptile denoted luck and symbolized divine wisdom. When Lizard appears, we can observe the symbols that come to us in sleep and decipher the deeper meanings that arrive from our inner knowing.

One of the more unusual traits that Lizard exhibits is the ability to shed its tail when attacked. When grabbed, the reptile swiftly scampers away, leaving its tail still twitching to distract the predator. The marvelous protective power this Animal Guide symbolizes is an ability to speedily safeguard oneself in the face of danger. As we learn to expertly hone this power we can easily transform our plight into a position of security.

Power

+ You thrive in warm climates and hate the cold. Those who embrace Lizard as their Animal often live in tropical or desert places or like to visit these landscapes often.

+ A deeply sensitive soul, you are greatly affected by your surroundings and the energy of others.

+ Innately aware of your gift for self-reflection, you enjoy engaging in meditation and visualization practices regularly.

+ You are endowed with a great capacity for heightened intuition, as well as an uncanny ability to discern messages from dreams.

Protection

+ When you feel vulnerable and exposed, know that you can go inward to connect with your true essence. Emerge with a greater awareness of your authentic self.

+ Use your innate sensitivity to safely guide you to your deeper truths. Allow yourself to feel protected by this quiet strength.

Wisdom

+ Your body is a powerful resource. Draw on your unique skills to create a sense of confidence.

- Look within. Trust your sensitive awareness to guide you.

- Dare to be who you truly are. Grace the world with your authenticity.

Messages from Lizard

Now is an excellent time to plan a vacation to a warm location. Explore options in tropical or desert parts of the world.

When Lizard appears, reflect on ways to develop stronger boundaries. Assess your current relationships and notice how they enliven or deplete your energy.

Are you going along with the status quo when you would rather be expressing your individuality? Allow your authenticity to emerge, and proudly display your true colors.

Observe the deeper meanings in dream symbols. Keep a dedicated journal to record details from your nighttime journeys.

IX

Bat

Inner Vision, Fearlessness, Change

The energy of Bat is often associated with darkness and fear. Their ability to see at night allows them to navigate through the shadows with ease. As an Animal Guide, this translates into a powerful energy of inner vision—the ability to see what others do not. When we reflect on Bat's unusual habit of sleeping upside down, we can understand how looking at things from a different perspective is one of the gifts it shares as an Animal ally. The fear that might be present as we explore new points of view transmutes into courage, as we begin to see clearly whatever helps us to grow.

There is much lore told about Bat and its messages of transformation. In Mayan, Oaxacan, and Nigerian cultures, Bat was viewed as a symbol for death. As an Animal Guide, this signifies rebirth through the ending of old ways. Sometimes, this becomes manifest as a fear of moving into unknown territory. Often, we feel it most intensely right at the edge of change. Chinese and indigenous North American elders recognized this as a powerful quality and revered Bat as a symbol of positivity in the face of darkness.

Bat is everywhere, yet rarely seen. There are more than a thousand species worldwide, ranging in size from as small as a bumblebee to as large as a bald eagle. It is a truly powerful creature, being the only mammal that can fly. Flight always signifies ascension to higher truths. When you are greeted by Bat there is a rising force present, which pushes boundaries and activates new ways of being.

The role of Bat in nature as a flower pollinator is a beautiful example of its skills of transformation.

Collecting the fine substance from the freshest blooms and distributing it to create new life is a powerful metaphor for Bat energy. When Bat emerges in our lives, we can reflect on how we can gather what we need in order to create positive change.

Power

+ You have an uncanny ability to initiate and adapt to change.

+ You possess a gift for success through transformation. Allowing yourself to release negative habits and embrace positive practices is easy for you.

+ You have strong intuition and are able to clearly see and feel things that others do not. This makes you naturally skilled at guiding others to new insights about themselves.

+ Bat essence is a potent source for those who work as healers, counselors, writers, and artists.

+ You are courageous and unafraid to convey your unique perspectives and share your magical gifts.

Protection

+ Be cautious of negative energy coming from others. Remember that you can remove yourself from a situation if it feels dangerous.

+ Your inner strength will guide you in breaking ties with those you no longer wish to be in a relationship with.

+ When you feel fear arise, you can create a sense of safety by connecting with your intuition. What do you know to be true?

Wisdom

- Trust that you are able to create change within yourself. Remember that the greatest growth comes at the darkest hour.

- Release what no longer serves you, as you welcome new opportunities. This paves the way for new wisdom to emerge.

- Your ability to see things from a different angle contributes to your spiritual evolution.

- Courage comes from trusting in yourself. Your instincts are your best guidance.

- Embrace your gifts of transcendence, as you rise above any obstacles in your path.

Messages from Bat

There is an important change on the horizon. Observe what is going on around you to reveal how best to navigate this transition.

Reflect on what you would like to do differently in your life. Is there something that you would like to change, that you are fearful of initiating?

Is there an area of your life where you currently feel stuck? Try shifting your perspective to discover the answers to a perplexing question.

Bat energy is most active at night, therefore the signs and symbols that arise in dreams are powerful clues for transformation.

Cat

Mystery, Aloofness, Clairvoyance

C at has been one of the most widely embraced Animal Guides since the beginning of human history. Ancient civilizations held this mysterious animal as a confidant, mentor, and guide. Stories from every culture feature Cat as a trusted "familiar" of witches, wizards, and magicians, blessed with the uncanny gift of extrasensory perception. Those who regard Cat as their Animal can feel an intangible presence even when their mystical counterpart cannot be seen. This is related to their ability to sense messages arriving from paranormal realms and a gift for interpreting the deeper meanings that surface within this supernatural space.

Cat has binocular vision and the ability to see in color, but this nocturnal animal's eyesight is especially powerful in the dark. The trait of enhanced sight is a metaphor for the gift of heightened intuition. This Animal Guide offers the ability to connect with the signs and symbols from soulful depths. Those who embrace Cat energy trust the mystical insights received, their inner knowing conveyed with a clarity that engenders true wisdom.

A solitary creature, preferring the night, Cat is elusive and typically cautious before trusting in new partnerships. Anyone who has ever bonded with Cat knows this finicky being's special selection process. Usually drawn to one member of a family, the animal coaxes us near with soft fur and sweet purrs. Chosen by this aloof loner to play a role in its life, we feel honored and gladly take part. When Cat bestows companionship upon us, we can be certain that this Animal Guide will lead us to understand concealed parts of ourselves that previously felt out of reach.

We've all heard the old adage that Cat has "nine lives," as it continually finds trouble yet prevails over peril. Extraordinary physical prowess contributes to Cat's success story. A voracious hunter in the wild, equipped with razor-sharp focus and agility, Cat homes in on its desired outcome and emerges victorious. When we observe this graceful being atop an elevated location surveying the landscape, we witness the power of exceptional attention. As an Animal Guide this denotes a dynamic ability to set high goals for oneself and achieve them using quick wit and deft skill.

Power

• You possess a special gift for being able to connect with your intuition and implicitly trust your inner knowing. The energy of Cat guides you to your natural source of heightened perception and clairvoyance.

• You are especially talented at focusing on your goals with clarity and certainty. You achieve success through a balance of strong physical and mental capacities.

• A typical introvert attuned to the darkness, you feel most alive in the nighttime hours. You prefer privacy and often hide out alone in secret places.

• Your somatic prowess is apparent in your agile movements. Those who embrace Cat energy make excellent dancers, yoga instructors, and martial-arts practitioners.

Protection

- When your sense of safety is challenged, either emotionally or physically, go inward to access your supreme inner sanctuary. Relax into the quietude and peace of this serene security.

- When you are confused and seek answers to difficult questions, take some time to reflect inwardly. Know that you can trust your intuition to guide you in the right direction.

Wisdom

- From resolution to reality, success begins with focused intention.

- Balance time alone with time spent with loved ones.

- Relax into your inner knowing.

- Embrace the great mystery of life.

Messages from Cat

When Cat energy is near, reflect on your current goals. Refocus your intentions and reassess your strategies.

Have you been keeping to yourself more than usual lately? Pick up the phone and reach out to a friend or family member in order to stay connected with those you care for.

Now is the perfect time to strengthen your powers of intuition. Explore metaphysical books, tarot decks, crystals, and guided meditation practices.

Otter

Persistence, Skill, Nurturance

A being that lives primarily in water, Otter teaches us much about our primordial wisdom. This might relate to our natural instincts for caring for children or connecting more deeply with our intuitive nature. Those who hold Otter as their Animal are at their best when they are involved in pursuits associated with the energies of nurturance, creativity, and inner wisdom. From the deep waters of life, Otter can guide us towards our true sources of power that have been submerged for too long.

Unusual creatures that live in water as well as on land, Otter spends half of its time hunting and devouring its prey. The remainder is spent sleeping, grooming, or mating. Even when they are engaged in the daily activities of life, they do so in a playful manner. When we observe the lively antics of this mammal, we can learn to accept this part of ourselves more deeply. Taking time to balance our work with fun is a gift this Animal Guide shares with us.

For decades, Otter was hunted for its skin and nearly exterminated as a result. Yet, the animal perseveres. Otter uses inventive techniques to navigate life's challenges. We see this illustrated in the way Otter wraps itself in kelp strands to secure its body while sleeping, or in the way rocks are expertly used as tools for cracking open a dinner of crab. This denotes skillfulness and a powerful capacity to deftly use various tools.

Otter energy is that of organization. Their homes are kept quite orderly, with various areas split up for different uses. Those who relate to Otter as their Animal make cheerful homeowners and loving parents. This can be seen in the ways in which Otter mothers single-handedly care for their young for the first six months of life. They nurse infants several times a day while floating on their backs, and quickly teach them to swim and hunt. This symbolizes an ability to create a safe, well-run home for family.

Power

+ You are skillful at using your resources inventively to create unique solutions.

+ Your persistence contributes to your success in meeting your goals.

+ You are inherently in tune with your divine essences of nurturance, intuition, and creativity.

+ You are organized and efficient in all your endeavors.

+ You have a lively nature and are at home in the rollicking tides of life. Riding the waves, you embrace playful joy like no other.

Protection

+ When you are faced with challenges and feel defeated, elaborate on your gift for patience. As you hang back, you can shift your perspective, then return to the task with a fresh outlook on how to prevail.

+ To alleviate boredom, allow yourself to go outside and play. Take a swim in the river or frolic on the beach with friends— just for fun.

+ When you're feeling scattered and unable to concentrate, take time to assess your space. Clear out clutter and reorganize in order to create peace of mind.

Wisdom

- Never lose hope. Take a break and return with a new perspective.

- Dive into deep waters in order to find pearls of wisdom.

- An organized space creates a peaceful mind.

Messages from Otter

When Otter drifts into your life, consider making
that big purchase you've been contemplating.
Make sure your finances are in order before you splurge.

Now is a good time to declutter
and reorganize your home or office.

Evaluate what you can do to initiate more play.
What really brings you joy?
Make a commitment to allow more time for fun.
When Otter emerges, reflect on your ability to listen
to your intuition. Are you following what you
know to be true on the inside?

Acknowledgments

With adoration for my furry companions, Honey, Koa, and Aesir, who fill my days with wonderment and joy. With immense gratitude to Ted Andrews, a pioneer in the field of animal energy, whose wisdom continues to inspire me. With boundless appreciation to my editors Zara Larcombe and Andrew Roff, for their encouragement and easeful presence in guiding me through the process of creating a beautiful book.

With love and gratitude for my family, Maximum Blue, Isra Om, Amanda, Audrey, and Winnie, whose belief in me always helps me to achieve my highest goals. To David, who is always willing to explore the mysteries of nature with me, I am ever grateful for his love and support. With eternal awe and gratitude for the Animal Spirits that revealed their brilliant essences to me so that I could translate their messages within these pages.

About the author

Dina Saalisi is a holistic healer with skills as Master Flower Essence Practitioner, a Board-Certified Health and Wellness Coach, Certified Hypnotherapist, educator, and empath. She is an energeticist with an extraordinary gift for connecting with the many facets of life-force energy, and her system of healing is grounded in reverence for nature and the nourishment provided from this universal source. She lives in California with her family and two pups. http://dinasaalisi.com

First published in Great Britain in 2022
by Laurence King Publishing
an imprint of The Orion Publishing Group Ltd
Carmelite House, 50 Victoria Embankment
London EC4Y 0DZ

An Hachette UK Company

10 9 8 7 6 5 4 3 2 1

© Text 2022 Dina Saalisi
Illustrations by Hsiao-Ron Cheng
Commissioning editor: Zara Larcombe
Senior Editor: Andrew Roff
Designer: Florian Michelet

The moral right of Dina Saalisi to be identified
as the author of this work has been asserted in
accordance with the Copyright, Designs and
Patents Act of 1988.

A CIP catalogue record for this book is
available from the British Library.

ISBN (Hardback) 978 1 9139 4767 5

Origination by FI Colour
Printed in China by C&C Offset Printing Co., Ltd

www.laurenceking.com
www.orionbooks.co.uk